WELCOME
Combat Vehicles

Modern military forces use combat vehicles to project their forces forward as well as carry-out reconnaissance and surveillance missions, while making sure that they develop protected platforms for an increasingly asymmetric theatre of warfare. Combat vehicles are an integral part of today's warfare, with light air-portable vehicles designed for advanced force operations and armoured platforms capable of protecting troops from roadside bombs. The history and development of these platforms spans back to World War Two and the introduction of the Willys jeep, used by Allied forces and adopted by Britain's SAS. They used it to mount operations against the Germans in North Africa and across Europe.

In the post-war years both the UK and US military produced new platforms to support missions in Korea, Vietnam, Panama, Malaya, Aden, Cyprus and Northern Ireland. The use of mines and improvised bombs by insurgents in the Malayan campaign resulted in ad hoc armour being fitted to British Land Rovers as a basic form of protection. When in Northern Ireland the threat increased, armoured panels were fitted to Land Rovers in a design that included a 'top cover' hatch allowing a soldier, wearing helmet and body armour, to scan the horizon during a patrol.

In 1991, the Gulf War saw a further evolution of combat platforms when US special forces introduced what was quickly dubbed the 'dune buggy'. These small, low-profile platforms,

fitted with heavy machine guns, were used in the western Iraqi desert in the hunt for Saddam Hussein's Scud missiles. Their success quickly saw the emergence of similar vehicles in the UK and among forces across NATO. The conflict in Afghanistan raised a requirement for light, bomb-protected combat vehicles that could be flown inside a Chinook and be capable of deploying in the desert for weeks. When US-led forces mounted the invasion of Iraq in 2003, the need for enhanced armoured vehicles was quickly identified. The Humvee spearheaded the invasion force but was found to be vulnerable to attack. It was upgraded and a series of bespoke 'protected' platforms built.

Today, NATO countries have opted for both fully protected vehicles that can carry specialist teams and fast, open platforms that can operate in all terrains. These light 'strike' platforms must be air-portable and capable of being dropped into action by parachute. The challenge for commanders has been to build 'armoured packages' to protect soldiers from roadside bombs and missiles while ensuring the driver and crew can maintain a clear view of the battlefield. More recent developments

include cameras and remote-controlled machine guns – allowing soldiers to remain protected and able to deliver firepower. As protected platforms get bigger, light vehicles used for 'behind the lines' raids and covert missions are getting smaller, to maintain a low radar footprint and maximise speed. Over the past decade these vehicles have been deployed by coalition forces in Iraq, Afghanistan and across the Middle East.

In an era when military capabilities and strategic operations are inextricably linked with cutting-edge technology and innovation, the need for modern combat vehicles fitted with what is called 'new warfighter' protection is paramount. The term 'combat vehicles' refers to any platform on the battlefield, from heavy armoured tanks to small strike vehicles. *Combat Vehicles* will detail the light and protected platforms used by both infantry and special operations units – some of which are tracked. In the 21st Century, as armies review the threat from drones and artificial intelligence, the requirement for small strike platforms and protected personnel carriers is paramount in the planning and execution of modern operations.

CONTENTS

06

34

CONTENTS

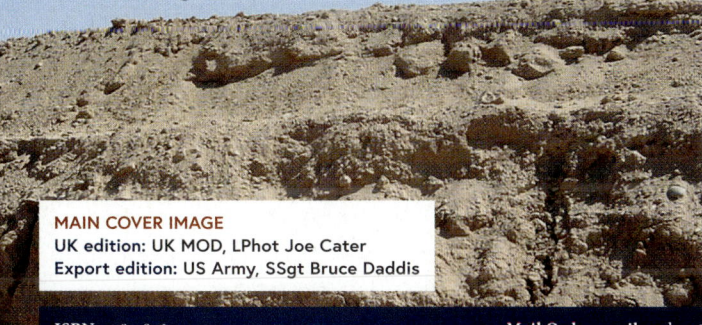

MAIN COVER IMAGE
UK edition: UK MOD, LPhot Joe Cater
Export edition: US Army, SSgt Bruce Daddis

ISBN: 978 1 83632 057 9
Editor: David Reynolds
Senior editor, specials: Roger Mortimer
Email: roger.mortimer@keypublishing.com
Cover Design: Steve Donovan
Design: SJmagic DESIGN SERVICES, India
Advertising Sales Manager: Sam Clark
Email: sam.clark@keypublishing.com
Tel: 01780 755131
Advertising Production: Becky Antoniades
Email: Rebecca.antoniades@keypublishing.com

SUBSCRIPTION/MAIL ORDER
Key Publishing Ltd, PO Box 300, Stamford, Lincs, PE9 1NA
Tel: 01780 480404
Subscriptions email: subs@keypublishing.com

Mail Order email: orders@keypublishing.com
Website: www.keypublishing.com/shop

PUBLISHING
Group CEO and Publisher: Adrian Cox

Published by
Key Publishing Ltd, PO Box 100, Stamford, Lincs, PE9 1XQ
Tel: 01780 755131 Website: www.keypublishing.com

PRINTING
Precision Colour Printing Ltd, Haldane, Halesfield 1, Telford, Shropshire. TF7 4QQ

DISTRIBUTION
Seymour Distribution Ltd, 2 Poultry Avenue, London, EC1A 9PU
Enquiries Line: 02074 294000.

Chapter One

THE DEVELOPMENT OF COMBAT VEHICLES

RIGHT: The Davidson armoured car which was designed on a Cadillac chassis and produced by Royal Page Davidson. War Office

BELOW: Combat vehicles deliver soldiers to their objectives – often across open terrain where they can be exposed to enemy fire, drone attacks or improvised explosive devices (IEDs). DPL

Combat vehicles deliver soldiers to their objectives – often across open terrain where they can be exposed to enemy fire, drone attacks or improvised explosive devices (IEDs). Protection for troops is critical in modern warfare. Fundamentally, combat vehicles are those that engage in operations in or around the forward edge of the battlefield. This also includes peace support and counterinsurgency operations, as well as intervention missions. While protection is a requirement when moving groups of soldiers through hostile environments, the need for unprotected 'open' platforms that are fast and can be shipped by helicopter remain a priority for specialist troops. In the 21st century, new evolving vehicle designs cover the spectrum of battlefield requirements, from reconnaissance to armoured fighting platforms. The future is already seeing vehicles which can operate remote control weapon systems and deploy drones to scout the area ahead of the force, as well as platforms that are fully autonomous. While most military platforms can be described

ABOVE: The British Husky was procured from the United States and deployed in Helmand. UK MoD

RIGHT: For much of history soldiers used horses – even elephants – to provide limited transport. One of the earliest forms of 'combat transport' was the Roman chariot. Museum of Rome

RIGHT: The White armoured car was produced by White Motors in Ohio and used by the American Expeditionary Force in 1918. War Office

as 'combat vehicles', military commanders view platforms, both wheeled and tracked, as critical to execute and sustain operations.

Roman Chariot

For much of history soldiers used horses – even elephants – to provide limited transport. One of the earliest forms of 'combat transport' was the Roman chariot. These wagons were initially used for racing, but by 2000 BC the light, horse-drawn, two-wheeled vehicles destined to revolutionise tactics appeared in Mesopotamia, Syria, and Turkey. The great advantage of the chariot was its speed, which permitted it to drive circles around a phalanx – a block of armed infantry standing to shoulder to shoulder in files several ranks deep. The chariot was expensive to produce and was often unsuitability across difficult terrain. In addition, each vehicle required a crew of two and sometimes three men – only one of whom actually handled offensive weapons and struck at the enemy.

Centuries later, the invention of the automobile allowed the military to develop a series of vehicles. It was this innovation that is often regarded as the origin of today's combat platforms. The invention of the tank took centre stage in World War One and at the same time nations across Europe generated wheeled and tracked designs as 'combat vehicles' to carry troops. The United States, Britain, »

ABOVE: The wartime Willys jeep soon became an iconic vehicle of World War Two. US DoD

ABOVE MIDDLE: In the post war years of the Cold War the then British War Office inspired by the success of the Willys jeep opted to develop their own combat vehicle to replace the Willys with the procurement of the newly developed Land Rover. Land Rover

Poland, Italy, France, Belgium. Hungry and Germany all built their own vehicles. America generated a series of small, armoured platforms built on the production chassis of cars. These included the Davidson armoured car which was designed on a Cadillac chassis and produced by Royal Page Davidson, an Illinois company – as well as the King armoured car, manufactured for the US Marine Corps (USMC). But these did not see action in World War One, although the White armoured car produced by White Motors in Ohio, was used by the American Expeditionary Force in 1918.

The British experimented with a range of ideas, many of which followed the same concept of using established car frames as the basis for their design. They included box-shaped vehicles such as the Peerless armoured car which was based on the frame of a lorry. Other early vehicles included the Lancaster, Delaunay-Belleville, as well as the Seabrook and Rolls-Royce armoured cars.

Belgium was the first nation to use armoured vehicles in combat with its Minerva vehicle deployed on the Western Front in 1914. Hungary built the Romfell which was based on a Mercedes chassis, with a crew of four and numerous mounted machine guns. The Canadian Defence department commissioned the Jeffrey armoured car, which was manufactured in Wisconsin. Some were exported to the UK and used by the British Army in India on the North-West Frontier. By now the French government had commissioned its automotive industry to build combat vehicles to support the French war effort.

Peugeot, Renault and Panhard rose to the task and were followed by the Italians, who turned to Lancia and Fiat, with the Ansaldo1Z platform incorporating a circular turret to enhance the gunner's vision. The Germans copied the Belgian Minerva using its design to deliver the Ehrhardt E-V/4. It was a heavily armoured truck with numerous weapon ports included. This platform saw operational service in the Baltic and the Western Front where mechanics made various conversions to the vehicles to meet the conditions. The most famous of these vehicles was the wartime Willys jeep. This was developed in 1940 after the US Army requested bids from car makers for a small, lightweight, four-wheel-drive vehicle to support the US Army, though it had no fixed weapons platforms. Willys-Overland, along with American Bantam and Ford, responded to the request and delivered the first prototype to the US Army in November 1940. When the US entered the war, production ramped up to meet the operational demands of the military.

Post War

In the post-war years of the Cold War, the then British War Office, inspired by the success of the Willys jeep, opted to develop their own combat vehicle to replace the Willys with the procurement of the newly developed Land Rover. The Land Rover brand was born in a sketch made in the sand on a Welsh beach in 1947 by the owners of Rover. While using a jeep on his farm in Anglesey,

RIGHT: Belgium was the first nation to use armoured vehicles in combat with its Minerva vehicle deployed on the Western Front in 1914. War Office

Rover's Technical Director Maurice Wilks and his brother Spencer Wilks, Rover's Managing Director, saw a gap in the market and development of Land Rover commenced using a jeep chassis and a Rover car engine. The use of simple body panels made from light alloy and a chassis fabricated from off-cuts avoided the use of rationed steel and the need for complex and expensive tools. The UK government purchased the Land Rover in an off-the-shelf procurement, a policy which was previously unheard of, and they proved highly successful when they entered service in 1949.

The UK military also sought a bespoke vehicle that was more suited to areas of operation where the UK Army served. Industry presented a series of potential contenders, and a contract was awarded to the Austin Champ Company to produce what the military called the 'truck quarter cargo' – although the name Champ stuck. The earliest Land Rovers were found to complement the Austin Champ very well. The Land Rover was cheaper, lighter, consumed less fuel, and was ideal for behind-the-lines transport duties. However, the Champ was regarded by some as a better suited as a front line combat vehicle, but its career was to be short-lived. The Austin Champ had a multi-fuel Rolls-Royce engine, which many believed was overpowered and consequently expensive to operate. The Champ could go as fast forwards as backwards, wade in depths of up to 3ft of water in an unprepared state and 6ft when 'prepared for wading'. Champs were also designed to carry

telephone line-laying equipment and there was a field ambulance variant with two stretchers. While the Champ delivered an excellent cross-country performance, it cost £1,200 per vehicle. It offered immense power

but was seen as over-engineered and the order of 15,000 was quicky cut to 4,000. The British Army found that for most general-purpose uses, the Land-Rover at half the cost of the Champ could do 80% of >>

ABOVE: The UK military also sought a bespoke vehicle, the Austin Camp, commanders felt it was more suited to areas of operation where the UK Army was serving. Austin Motors

LEFT: The Land Rover made a major contribution to the UK's war effort in the 1991 Gulf war, but there was still no dedicated light platform or vehicle that could withstand IEDs. DPL

LEFT: In early 1950 a basic armoured personnel carrier built by Humber and dubbed the 'Pig' by soldiers was introduced to provide protection to soldiers. DPL

the Austin's work. Raw economics sealed the Champ's fate – it was far too expensive and was consigned to history. Hence, the Land Rover took centre stage as the most developed combat platform with variants developed for desert terrain, command and communication, and as an ambulance variant. The vehicle saw extensive exports sales across the globe – including to the US military.

In early 1950 a basic armoured personnel carrier was built by the UK company Humber and introduced to provide protection to soldiers. A basic design, it delivered exactly what it was designed for and remained in service through the conflict in Northern Ireland as a troop carrier. Dubbed the 'Pig', it was supported by a more refined armoured personnel carrier called the Saracen. Designed and produced by Alvis, the latter served from 1952 to 1976 and became a familiar sight on operations in Ulster. Besides the driver and commander, a squad of eight soldiers plus a troop commander could be carried. Most models were fitted with a small turret on the roof, carrying a Browing .30 machine gun. A .303 Bren gun could also be mounted on an anti-aircraft ring mount accessed through a roof hatch and there were ports on the sides through which troops could fire. It was removed from active service in the 1970s after extensive service in Ulster where it became a familiar sight and had been nicknamed 'Sixers'.

By the end of the 1950s the British Army identified a requirement for a light armoured reconnaissance vehicle and after a series of

evaluations, the Daimler car company produced the Ferret Scout Car which remained in service until the 1970s. It was a two-crew platform developed from the wartime Dingo and saw service in Cyprus, Malaya, Northern Ireland and the 1991 Gulf War. In 1959 the Saladin entered service with the British Army. This heavy 11-tonne armoured car was used throughout the Cold War, in Aden and in Northern Ireland – it had a reputation for excellent reliability in the desert – before it too was retired in the 1970s.

Innovations

Meanwhile, as the US continued with the Willys jeep, the UK mounted a trial with the Citroen 2CV as the Ministry of Defence

sought a light air-portable vehicle which could be airlifted ashore from the fleet's aircraft carriers by the newly introduced helicopter. The end-user for the vehicle was the Royal Marines which had mounted the world's first helicopter assault at Suez in 1956. Now they selected the French car principally for its lightweight, front-wheel drive, and basic load carrying capability which made it ideal to be airlifted by the early Wessex helicopters. Prior to being flown ashore, doors, windows and roof canopy were removed. The plan was that they would land ready to operate, carrying radios, rations and ammunition. Analysts suggested that their incredible suspension meant they were ideal to withstand repeated

LEFT: New upgrades were developed with the Land Rover WMIK (weapon mounted installation kit) being widely used on operations. UK MoD

BELOW LEFT: The UK mounted a trial with the French Citroen 2CV as the Ministry of Defence sought a light air-portable vehicle which could be airlifted ashore from the fleet's aircraft carriers. UK MoD

BELOW: The Royal Navy used the 2CV as an interim 'light platform' which could be flown ashore to provide mobility for the commander's radio net. DPL

heavy underslung landings from helicopters from up to 10ft above the ground. In reality, pilots were directed to land their underslung loads by naval air parties who talked the pilots and their loads into position before two soldiers would release the load – in some circumstances the aircrew would control the despatch. The 2CVs were also limited in that they could not carry any significant payload, but despite their limitations, a small number saw service in Borneo during the Indonesian confrontation of 1963-66. This innovative use of this commercial car caught the attention of strategic planners in Whitehall who identified a requirement for a lighter, air-portable combat vehicle that could be carried inside a transport plane, ferried by helicopter as well as dropped by parachute, and be deployed wherever it was needed around the world. Land Rover quickly developed the Lightweight or air-portable variant; a smaller and narrower vehicle compared to the standard Land Rover. It was produced from 1968 to 1984.

The Land Rover has for decades been Britain's iconic military combat vehicle. After initial introduction to service, modifications were made which included 'blackout' lights, the installation of heavy-duty suspension, upgrades to the brakes, the fitting of a 24V electrics, convoy lights, new electronic suppression of the ignition system, as well as mounts for machine guns. The Land Rover was used across the armed forces for a wide range of tasks with every infantry battalion in the British »

LEFT: In the mid-1960s British forces were embarked on a counterinsurgency in Aden and deployed the Land Rovers to support mobile patrols. UK MoD

LEFT: A Land Rover in Northern Ireland with no armoured protection supported by four Humber 'Pigs' during a riot. DPL

BELOW: Land Rover quickly developed the Lightweight or air-portable – a smaller and narrower vehicle than the standard Land Rover. Seen here disembarking from a landing craft, it served across the globe with UK forces. DPL

By the late 1990s Land Rover had introduced the WMIK (weapon mounted installation kit). Its format consisted of a driver, a commander and gunner with heavy machine gun, which was used for vehicle protection. The WMIK was deployed on operations in Sierra Leone and would later serve in Iraq and Afghanistan. But in 2000, Rover Group was broken up by BMW and Land Rover was sold to the Ford Motor Company, becoming part of its Premier Automotive Group. Jaguar Land Rover has been a subsidiary of Tata Motors since they founded it as a holding company for the acquisition of Jaguar Cars and Land Rover from Ford in 2008.

New concepts

The 1970s had seen the emergence of the Scimitar vehicle – a light tracked platform with a 30mm Rarden cannon. Fast and reliable, it was the perfect armoured reconnaissance asset with deployments across the globe. With the Bandvagn BV202 came the first variant of the specialist combat vehicle that was developed

ABOVE: The WMIK was deployed on operations in Sierra Leone and would later serve in Iraq and Afghanistan. Dil Banerjee/DPL

RIGHT: Land Rovers made a major contribution to UK operations in the 1991 Gulf War where their performance was spotted by the US Rangers. Bob Morrison

Army operating dozens of 'Landys' as they were sometimes called. By the mid 1960s these platforms were used as a platform for anti-tank weapons, surface-to-air missiles, and heavy machine guns. It was upgraded with a long wheelbase version, a lighter model for air-mobility and enhanced platforms for special forces. These reliable vehicles were dropped by parachute on what the RAF called medium-stressed platforms, flown into action by helicopter and driven off landing craft in amphibious operations.

In the mid-1960s, British forces were embarked on a counterinsurgency in Aden and deployed the Land Rovers to support mobile patrols. To improve access for soldiers, the doors and roofs were removed, allowing those onboard to have improved vision. The same policy was adopted in Northern Ireland when UK forces were sent in to restore calm after sectarian riots in 1969. But within a few years the open-topped Land Rovers were seen as a liability as protestors were able to throw bricks and coffee jar bombs and shoot at the soldiers who had no protection. By the 1980s a decision had been made to upgrade the majority of Land Rovers deployed in Ulster with armoured panels to provide protection from bombs and bullets. This was perhaps a pioneering move that eventually influenced the British and US military towards protected mobility for combat vehicles.

In the 1991 Gulf War Land Rovers made a major contribution and were in action again in both Iraq and Afghanistan. The Land Rover has been exported across the globe and in late 1990s the vehicle was upgraded. The 'Snatch' Land Rover

had been developed for operations in Northern Ireland and was later to serve in Iraq and Afghanistan. The company then developed the Defender and the Wolf variants.

RIGHT: A British Snatch Land Rover heads a convoy of Coalition vehicles in Iraq. US DoD

for operations in the arctic and used
by the UK and most NATO forces.
By 1991 new developments in combat
vehicles emerged in the Gulf War
with the development of what were
called 'dune buggies'. These small
three-man vehicles were fast, heavily
armed and could be airlifted by
helicopter and transport plane. In
Iraq's western desert these platforms
were used to hunt Saddam Hussein's
Scud missile sites. Other variants
include the Desert Patrol Vehicle and
adapted Humvees.

In the UK, the military procured
the Longline Light Strike Vehicle.
This new combat vehicle was
assigned to the UK's 24th Airmobile
Brigade and regularly deployed in
NATO exercises – although the initial
order was never extended. A second,
more protected platform called the
Saxon, was ordered to support
the infantry. It was deployed »

ABOVE: A British Land Rover from a reconnaissance unit pictured in Kuwait at the end of the war. David Reynolds /DPL

ABOVE RIGHT: The Humvee was the main combat vehicle of the US military and underwent a major upgrade in Iraq as shown. US DoD

RIGHT: The British Longline Light Strike Vehicle which could be airlifted by helicopter and carried Milan anti-tank weapons. David Reynolds /DPL

in Northern Ireland, Bosnia, and Kosovo but its poor handling ended its career, and it was withdrawn from service. In 1992, the US Army's Rangers identified a need for a new defensive vehicle and selected the Land Rover Special Operations department to develop what was called the Ranger Special Operations Vehicle (RSOV). The decision to adopt the vehicle was inspired by American commanders after seeing the Land Rover deployed in the 1991 Gulf War. They noted that the vehicle was easier to use in desert terrain compared to the heavier Humvee and, while it had little protection, it was air portable. In total 60 RSOVs were initially purchased to fulfil a

requirement for 12 per battalion. The US Rangers secretly deployed the vehicle to support potential anti-terrorist efforts and to ensure the safety of people visiting the 1992 Olympics in Spain, but they were kept out of the public eye. At

the same time, the USMC invested in a jeep-style platform called the Growler designed specifically for use with the V-22 Osprey tiltrotor aircraft. These small jeeps have an obvious 'Willys' look and are used by the USMC as a utility vehicle in

ABOVE LEFT: Light Strike vehicles could easily be flown forward by Black Hawk and Chinook helicopters. DPL

ABOVE RIGHT: By the 1980s a decision had been made to upgrade the majority of Land Rovers deployed in Ulster with armoured panels to provide protection from bombs and bullets. David Reynolds/DPL

almost any environment or terrain. A second platform called the 'Badger' was designed for the Corps to operate with the V-22 Osprey, but wars in Iraq and Afghanistan, which had erupted at the start of 2000s, were now demanding new concepts in combat vehicles.

Protected Mobility

The 2001 intervention in Afghanistan saw the deployment of NATO forces on peace support operations in Kabul. The capital quickly faced a number of threats from insurgents, in the wake of the Taliban's demise, who were hiding in the shadows. Attacks on NATO followed and the requirement for

light, bomb-protected combat vehicles was seen as an urgent priority. France deployed the VAB, a small, armoured personnel carrier, while Italian forces used the Iveco light armoured platform. Both the US and UK, who led the 2001 intervention, had limited 'combat vehicles' capable of providing crew protection. The British opted to return to using soft skinned vehicles – Land Rovers and the newer Pinzguager. Then in 2003, the invasion of Iraq saw the US military reliant on the Humvee as the backbone of their invasion force. It fell victim to enemy attack as insurgents launched Rocket Propelled Grenades (RPGs) and

mounted Improvised Explosive Devices (IEDs). The British Land Rover also fell victim to attacks, forcing both the US and UK to quickly launch projects to develop a series of protected vehicles. As the US and UK expanded the conflict in Afghanistan, Washington developed a protected combat vehicle to meet a range of threats. These new vehicles included the Cougar and Caiman which delivered enhanced armoured protection to ground forces. The British Snatch Land Rover and the BV206, known as the Viking, were sent to Iraq and later Afghanistan, and were quickly found to be vulnerable. The UK purchased numerous protected combat platforms from the US, including the renamed Mastiff, which was regarded by troops on the ground as the ultimate protection. But it sacrificed speed and manoeuvrability, leaving them bordering on logistics platforms. Other innovations procured by the UK military for operations in Helmand included the Warthog armoured tracked and the much smaller protected patrol vehicles such as the Foxhound, Husky and Panther. Since the introduction of the combat vehicle to the battlefield in World War Two, the combat vehicle had matured into a bespoke platform thanks to the proven capability of the iconic Willys jeep.

RIGHT: In late 2006 the Royal Marines deployed the BV tracked utility vehicle to Afghanistan, but its protection was limited. UK MoD

LEFT: The Snatch Land Rover was designed for operations in Northern Ireland and was later deployed to Iraq and Afghanistan. Dil Banerjee /DPL

Chapter Two

THE WILLYS JEEP

RIGHT: The Willys jeep in desert colours for operations in the North African desert, pictured at an anniversary display in France. US DoD

The catalyst for the development of combat vehicles was the iconic Willys jeep, developed in the United States at the start of World War Two which served as the ultimate battlefield taxi for Allied forces across campaigns in North Africa, Europe, and the Pacific. Its lightweight frame allowed it to be dropped by parachute and landed by glider, with the most notable operations being the invasion of France at Normandy and the airborne assault at Arnhem in June and September 1944.

The Willys jeep was powerful, robust, easy to maintain and hugely versatile on the battlefield. More than 600,000 variants of the all-terrain vehicle were manufactured in factories across America between 1941 and 1945. It was seen everywhere and quickly generated a reputation for reliability with both US and Allied forces. Officially termed the quarter-tonne jeep, it was hailed by US President Dwight D Eisenhower as a war-winning item of equipment. They were so in demand that they were even supplied to the Soviets to help in their

BELOW: Hundreds of Willys jeeps were deployed to Normandy as part of Operation Overlord. War Office

campaign against the Germans. The British Army also used the jeep, and the newly formed Special Air Service adopted it to mount attacks on the Germans across the North African desert and in Europe. In the post-war years, it went on to serve in both the Korean War and Vietnam.

Made to order

In July 1940, the US War Department approached a number of car manufacturers, inviting bids for a tender to produce a light utility reconnaissance vehicle to replace the motorcycles, sidecars, Model T Fords, and horses that had been used in World War One, which had been limited in what they could carry and unable to operate in heavy mud. The proposed new vehicle needed to be four-wheel drive, have a high ground clearance, weigh less than 1200lb and have the ability to transport

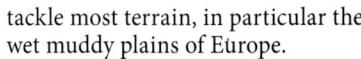

tackle most terrain, in particular the wet muddy plains of Europe.

By early October 1941, it became clear that Willys-Overland could not keep up with the increasing demand of orders, so Ford received government contracts to build 30,000 jeeps. An extra condition to the Ford agreement was to manufacture them in several different assembly plants in addition to Ford's main River Rouge facility in Michigan, with vehicles also being produced in Texas and California. Ford built its jeeps with functionally interchangeable parts and components that were already available. One minor but useful change that Ford made was to replace the welded front grille with a single sheet of pressed steel with nine vertical open slots to increased ventilation to the radiator. Willys also adopted this in their production of what became known as the MB but, predictably, there were still many minor differences: the Ford chassis had an inverted U-shaped front »

RIGHT: The US developed and designed the Willys jeep at a re-enactment event – it was the catalyst for today's combat vehicles. US DoD

RIGHT: British airborne troops unload a Willys jeep and trailer from a glider at Normandy in June 1944. War Office

BELOW RIGHT: The jeep underwent dramatic testing to ensure it could sustain operations across undulating terrain. US DoD

BELOW: A wounded US Marine is evacuated on a Willys jeep during the war in the Pacific. US DoD

three soldiers and a 700lb payload. Companies were given just 11 days to submit their proposals, deliver a prototype in 49 days and have a vehicle ready in 75 days. Just three companies responded: Ford, Willys-Overland and Bantam.

While the Bantam met the brief, the War Department also liked the look of Willys-Overland's offering. The Willys was designed in 75 days and had both two- and four-wheel drive capability, with a four-cylinder 60hp engine, but it weighed 2,200lb. It had six forward speeds and two reverse speeds, with a top speed of 55mph. In addition, the versatile jeep could pull anti-tank guns, howitzers and was able to ford streams or flooded areas in water up to 40in. The first prototype arrived with the US Army in November 1940. By July 1941, the US War Department wanted to standardise production and decided to select a single manufacturer to supply them with the next order for 16,000 vehicles. Willys won the contract due to its powerful 60hp engine and lower unit cost, with certain design features from the Bantam and Ford entries incorporated, moving it from what was designated an 'MA' to an 'MB'. The most obvious feature was the flat

bonnet or hood, while the headlights were moved away from the fenders to avoid potential damage, with changes also made to the front grille. Four-wheel drive allowed the vehicle to

ABOVE: Willys jeeps lead a small convoy away from the beaches at Normandy after the seaborne landings in 1944. War Office

ABOVE MIDDLE: General Eisenhower hailed the Willys as a war winning item of equipment. US DoD

RIGHT: Some of the jeeps flown into Normandy with the 6th Airborne Division were destroyed when the gliders crashed. War Office

crossmember instead of a tubular bar and a Ford-script letter 'F' was stamped onto many small parts.

What's in a name

The word 'jeep' was used well before World War Two when soldiers referred to raw recruits or other personnel who had yet to prove their mettle in combat as 'jeeps'. It was also used by military motor mechanics as slang for new, unproven vehicles and prototypes that arrived on the battlefield.

In 1936, the cartoonist EC Segar named a character in his *Popeye* comic strip as 'Eugene the Jeep'. This character was able to go anywhere, walk through walls and move between dimensions, achieving the impossible. Eugene the Jeep's go-anywhere ability resulted in various industrial and four-wheel drive vehicles getting nicknamed the 'jeep'. Around 1940, converted tractors supplied to the US Army as prime movers for stores and logistics were named 'jeeps' and Halliburton used the name for an electric logging device.

In World War Two, soldiers initially dubbed the Dodge Reconnaissance vehicle as the 'jeep', with the three-quarter tonne Command Cars later called 'beeps' (as in 'big jeeps', while the smaller quarter-tonne cars were called 'peeps' as in 'son of jeeps.')

The 1940s terminology is summed up in a definition given in a book held in the Pentagon library and titled *Words of the Fighting Forces* by Clinton Sanders. It states that a jeep is "a four-wheel drive car of one-half to one-and-one-half tonne capacity for reconnaissance or other army

RIGHT: US President Dwight D Eisenhower. Pentagon

FAR RIGHT: The Germans designed a four-wheel drive amphibious vehicle for their Army called the Schwimmwagen. US DoD

LEFT: A British Army Willys leads a Sherman tank at Monte Cassino. War Office

duty. A term applied to the bantam cars, and occasionally to other motor vehicles."

Operational service

The United States provided jeeps to almost all Allied forces in World War Two. Britain, Canada, Australia, India, the Free French, USSR, and China, all received them, mostly under the American Lend-Lease agreement, with more than 182,500 units being distributed to the Allies. The jeep was used in North Africa, was landed at D-Day in France and operated with the Chindits (long range penetration groups) in Burma. It also landed with the assault waves in the Philippines and Okinawa, as well as carrying the victorious Allies into Rome, Paris, Berlin, and Tokyo. In the European theatre, they were so commonplace that some German troops believed that each American soldier was issued with his own jeep.

The jeep's flat hood was often used as a commander's map table, a chaplain's field altar, a soldiers' poker table and to evacuate injured troops. When the United States entered the war in 1941, production ramped up to meet the operational demands of the military. The US Army assigned 144 jeeps to each infantry regiment, while others were used by the artillery, medical units, reconnaissance and as command vehicles. Across Europe, the Willys jeep was used in almost every campaign. Eisenhower, the supreme commander of the Allied Expeditionary Force in Europe, had a great fondness for the jeep. He described it "as a decisive weapon of World War Two" when he famously commented that "the jeep, the Dakota and the landing craft were the three tools that won

LEFT: Commandos of the Special Service Brigade with a pedal bike fitted on the bonnet. US DoD

BELOW: A Willys in the ambulance role, with the stretcher on the roof. US DoD

Jeeps with the SAS

Britain's elite Special Air Service (SAS) used the Willys jeep to spearhead its campaign of behind-the-line's raids against German positions, hitting vital Nazi supply lines and airfields. The jeep was the perfect platform to mount their twin Vickers machines guns, which were key in the missions against Erwin Rommel's desert forces. The SAS packed their jeeps with extra ammunition, food, and water to support their long-range desert patrols. In some situations, soldiers modified the jeeps by removing the windscreens or cutting bigger holes in the front grilles to get more airflow through the radiator. Fuel cans were packed on the side and rear of the jeep, with room left for just two soldiers.

Formed by David Stirling in 1941, the SAS was originally called the 'L' Detachment, with the 'L' designation to give the impression of a much bigger force as part of a British disinformation campaign to deceive

LEFT: In the Far East, the Gurkhas used the Willys with General Slim's force in Burma. War Office

BELOW: British Military Police crew a Willys jeep. War Office

the war." General George Marshall, Chief of Staff of the US Army, called the vehicle "America's greatest contribution to modern warfare."

Aircraft recognition symbols were initially painted on the bonnet or hood and were used for several years, although after 1942 most British jeeps did not have any markings. The star is often mistaken for a purely American symbol, whereas from mid-1943 onwards, all Allied vehicles were ordered to carry the bonnet star, with only a few exceptions. US army jeeps often had a US-designed rifle rack fitted on the inside of the windscreen and these were also found on a lot of British jeeps. Some, but not all, British jeeps carried pioneer tools – an axe and shovel.

Fuel cans were often fitted at the rear of the jeep, but some units on long-range patrols packed the rear seats with fuel containers. British metal fuel containers were copied from the German cans that contained an integral funnel as they were stronger and better made. Soldiers quickly dubbed the fuel containers as 'jerrycans' a term which is still used today.

After World War Two, the original jeep continued to serve but was upgraded and known as the M38 and deployed in the Korean War. In 1949, the M38A1 Willys MD arrived – the first Willys jeep with a significantly restyled body, immediately recognisable by its rounded bonnet and wheelarches. It was used by the US Army and adapted by many nations as a reconnaissance vehicle, fitted with anti-tank weapons or as an ambulance.

In addition to these, more than 12,000 amphibious jeeps were built by Ford in the early years of

World War Two, some of which were provided to the Soviet Union. Nicknamed the 'seep' ('sea jeep'), they were longer than the standard vehicle and struggled in muddy terrain, with their performance allegedly listed as "disappointing." The seeps had insufficient protection from waves on the open sea, which resulted in tragic losses during the Allied landings in Sicily in 1943. By contrast, the Austrian car designer and engineer Ferdinand designed a lighter four-wheel drive amphibious vehicle for the German Army called the Schwimmwagen, which quickly became popular with German soldiers due to its excellent off-road performance and reliability.

LEFT: The wartime British SAS adopted the Willys for their operations in North Africa. War Office

ABOVE: Two SAS Willys jeeps in France with the radiator covers removed. War Office

RIGHT: SAS soldiers often removed unneeded headlights, and the grille covers to make sure more air went into the radiator. War Office

BELOW: The jeep was found to be the perfect platform as spare fuel and supplies could be strapped to the bonnet. War Office

for four hours across the desert, often with a dozen or more jeeps in convoy, travelling under moonlight as there were no night-vision goggles or global positioning systems to rely on. It was these jeeps that provided the SAS with the ability to hit the enemy with speed and surprise. During an attack on Sirte in December 1941, the SAS and their colleagues in the Long-Range Desert Group (LRDG) developed the technique of driving their trucks at speed between the rows of aircraft, riddling the planes with machine guns and blowing up fuel dumps.

The SAS quicky learned enough from the LRDG to operate independently and used its own jeeps to attack Nazi airfields. Their Vickers K machines guns were bolted to the front chassis and could be fired by the passenger in the front right seat – the vehicles were all left-hand drive. After D-Day, the SAS took its jeeps deep inside occupied France and into Germany itself, harassing enemy troop movements and passing back reports about German positions to allow the RAF to bomb them. SAS soldiers famously named one of their jeeps as *Fuka* after an attack on an airfield in Egypt.

Special editions

In early 1941, the US Army's Tank Command was seeking to make their anti-tank guns more mobile and, by early 1942, the M3 artillery gun had been fitted on a pedestal mount and was being towed by the Willys jeep. Planners then fitted a 37mm anti-tank weapon on a Willys as part of an experimental trial, but the lightweight jeep was more suited to smaller guns or rockets. By 1945, the first large recoilless rifles had been fitted to the vehicle.

During Operation Varsity and the crossing of the Rhine, two 75mm rifles were fitted on jeeps for use in the anti-tank role, used by soldiers serving with the 17th US Airborne Division. To extend carrying capability, baggage racks were fitted, and tests were undertaken to extend the jeep. »

the Axis into thinking there was a full parachute regiment in north Africa preparing to hit German troops. The force had actually been conceived as a commando force to operate covert operations to cripple the German war effort and allow the Allies to counter-attack and progress into Europe.

The SAS initially consisted of five officers and 60 other ranks who operated on intelligence from the British headquarters in Cairo. They would drive

Several tracked jeep prototypes were built to meet the extreme environments in Alaska and Canada. This modification came after America had entered the war and the Japanese attack on the Aleutian Islands, which sit off Alaska and are owed by the United States. The Canadian Bombardier company and Willys created the T29 jeep half-track. It entered service in 1942 with an expanded rear chassis to include a total of six wheels – three on each side – with a broad rubber belt serving as a track, running around two Ford model A wheels, followed by a notably larger wheel at each back corner. Instead of front wheels, the rig was fitted with skis and the front-wheel driveline was removed to save cost and weight.

Some jeeps, especially in Europe, received limited 'ad-hoc' armour, which consisted of a rear slanting armour plate in front of the grille, replacing the windshield, as well as the sides. Numerous trials were undertaken to try and adapt the vehicle for other tasks. The most extreme was a plan to engineer a jeep that could be used as an autogyro. Designed by the Austrian helicopter engineer Raoul Hafner in 1942, this rotabuggy was first evaluated by the British Airborne Forces Experimental Establishment and seen as a concept to support the 1st and 6th Airborne Divisions. The design involved a rotor assembly fitted above the jeep's cabin, along with a lightweight tail for stabilisation. The plan was to tow the rotabuggy into the air by a bomber, in the same method as a glider would later be developed and towed, then the 'airborne jeep' would be released and land under its own power. But the arrival of a glider that

could carry jeeps and light guns and made the flying jeep superfluous.

The replacement

By the late 1970s, the US military was seeking a platform to replace the jeep. Washington had contracted Ford to redesign the jeep in the 1950s, which resulted in the M151. It followed the same concept of being compact, light enough to manhandle, low profile, with a folding windshield and was deployed widely on operations in Vietnam, Panama, and Grenada.

However, by the mid-1960s, it became obvious that it was time to re-evaluate the requirements for a replacement. In response to instructions to develop a new versatile vehicle for reconnaissance, FMC, a California company, presented its dune buggy to the army. It was called the XR 311 and was ready for testing in 1970, but commanders wanted a

RIGHT: A number of experimental jeeps evolved, including this tracked version. US DoD

platform that was more robust while being just as versatile.

By 1977, the US military implemented a new project to find a vehicle that could be used to perform a multitude of different functions, including troop carrier, light cargo transport, munitions carrier and an ambulance. This was the XM966 Combat Support Vehicle Program. Three companies responded with designs: AM General, Chrysler and Teledyne Continental. AM General was seen as a front-runner with its front engine design, high ground clearance, wide and versatile body and large diesel or gasoline V8 with plenty of torque. This new platform was listed as the High Mobility Multipurpose Wheeled Vehicle or Humvee, intended to replace a wide range of light vehicles used for transport and logistics.

The first prototype Humvee was built in 1979 and, after extensive checks and evaluation, including dropping the vehicle by parachute and

months of testing at the Aberdeen proving ground, the new platform was approved for production. The initial contract was for 55,000 vehicles over a five-year period and the first Humvees were delivered to the US Army

in 1985. The vehicle quickly proved its suitability to military operations. They were deployed for transport, reconnaissance, command and control and a variety of other tasks. Their mobility and versatility made them an invaluable asset to the US military who deployed the Humvee with US forces in Germany, South America, and the Pacific.

The Humvee quickly made an impact during the 1991 Gulf War, when it was used extensively by American forces in Kuwait and Iraq. The vehicle's ability to navigate the harsh desert terrain and carry troops and equipment across a challenging landscape was crucial to the success of the operation. But its lack of armour left it vulnerable to attack and US special operations units sought something smaller and more agile. Then after the US intervention in Somalia in 1993, where the Humvee was found to be vulnerable to rocket-propelled grenade attacks, a review was carried out to examine the vehicles' protection, which had not been designed to face heavy machine gun fire. The US led invasion of Iraq saw hundreds of Humvees operating across the desert in many variants, which included anti-tank operations, command and control, forward observation platforms and ambulances.

The high volume of asymmetric attacks launched by Iraqi insurgents left the Humvee vulnerable. Roadside bomb became a daily threat and at a rate that US planners had not expected. In the first four months of 2006, a total of 67 US soldiers were killed in Humvees while on operations in Iraq, many of them around Baghdad. To increase protection, Washington ordered enhanced armour kits for the vehicles, some of which were initially bolted on. The shape and design of protected and light vehicles was changing.

RIGHT: A trial was carried out to mount a small artillery gun on the rear of the jeep. US DoD

BELOW: The 'rocket jeep' proved successful, although it could not carry enough rockets to reload easily. US DoD

Chapter Three

CONFLICT SHAPES NEW
COMBAT VEHICLES

Military campaigns often influence new designs in vehicles to counter threats and enhance combat capability as troops face fresh challenges on the battlefield. Today, there are two main variants of the combat vehicle in service – the 'protected' platform to defend personnel against attack and the 'light' platform for operations in the urban environment.

Modern protected vehicles are routinely heavier vehicles, with armour incorporated as part of their design and production or added to factory delivered vehicles as part of a bespoke upgrade for service in counterinsurgency or hostile environments where the kinetic threat is high.

Light vehicles have little protection in order to guarantee speed and reduce their weight ratio to ensure they can be air-lifted by helicopter or dropped by parachute, with most of

these 'strike' platforms used by special operations and supporting arms.

The first focus on upgrading 'protected' vehicles came in the 1960s when British Army units deployed on a series of counter-insurgency operations in the Middle and Far East. Roll-bars were fitted to Land Rovers and other patrol vehicles to counter mine blasts. Later, composite armour was added to vehicles assigned to internal security operations before a full armour package was added as the design of vehicles changed.

The Challenge
The design of combat vehicles is based around the operational

requirement to protect and project troops across the battlefield. Protected vehicles provide safety against Improvised Explosive Devices (IEDs) but often lack speed. Light 'strike' platforms offer no protection – the priority being to reduce weight and size to deliver speed. Many of the new light vehicles being introduced present a radical new design in the shape of vehicles after almost two decades of experience on high-intensity operations.

In the initial 2001 deployment into Kabul by NATO, a lack of protected vehicles left Western soldiers exposed to bomb blasts. The Russians had experienced the same fate in Chechnya and more recently in Ukraine where an initial failure to deploy protected platforms left Moscow's forces vulnerable to attack. In areas such as Sudan both government and rebel forces have shaped their combat capability against limited **»**

BELOW: Throughout the 1970s and 80s, the Land Rover was widely used by British forces but offered little protection against mine blasts. DPL

LEFT: The first post-war focus on upgrading 'protected' vehicles came in the 1960s when British Army Land Rovers were fitted with rollbars to counter mine blasts. DPL

BOTTOM: The strategic focus in the 1990s was on high readiness forces who needed small strike vehicles that could be airlifted into action. DPL

BELOW: It wasn't until the early 2000s that vehicles were built with integral armoured protection and the ability to add packages, as the design of vehicles changed. US DoD

ABOVE: The profile of the Land Rover can be seen clearly in the design of the Israeli MDT David protected vehicle IDF

ABOVE MIDDLE: The US military M1301 Infantry Squad Vehicle is widely regarded as the most advanced light vehicle in service. US DoD

investment and often deployed pick-up trucks. In Syria, the intense level of warfare forced the warring factions to improvise their combat vehicles with sheets of steel welded to vehicles to deliver increased protection, while also using these bizarre-looking platforms to mount suicide bomb attacks.

The Israeli Defence Force (IDF) has adopted many of the lessons learnt over the past five decades and its main protected patrol platform, called the MDT David, is one of

a number of specialist combat vehicles used by the IDF. Worldwide, hundreds of different vehicles have been used for military service in both the protected and light roles. India claims to have the world's strongest and most protected patrol vehicle, the Kalyani M4, produced in South Africa and deployed in the country's border with China. However, the US-produced M1301 Infantry Squad Vehicle is widely regarded as the most advanced light vehicle in service.

The challenge for designers is to develop platforms that improve combat capability in protected vehicles that often have reduced vision for occupants on the battlefield, at the same time as shaping light vehicles that have little protection for them to remain under enemy radar.

Improved Protection
The need for 'protected' combat vehicles has been a recurring issue

RIGHT: The South African Kalyani M4 is in service with the Indian Army as part of its UN force and has been deployed on the border with China. UN

in counter-insurgency operations for UK forces since 1945. In Vietnam, US forces had experimented with vehicle protection, but it was mainly ad hoc.

By 1969, growing civil unrest in Northern Ireland had resulted in the British government sending troops onto the streets of Belfast and Londonderry in support of an exhausted Royal Ulster Constabulary, which had faced months of sectarian disturbances. The move left the military with very little time to

prepare for what was supposed to be a short-term mission. The British Army used Land Rovers that offered little protection against rioters armed with bricks, Molotov cocktails and so-called coffee jar bombs. By the early 1970s, many of these vehicles were retrofitted with a protection system called Makrolon. It was a glass-like reinforced plastic shield that encased vehicles in a light-weight polycarbonate mould that was resistant to petrol bombs, bricks, and low-calibre velocity rounds. Makrolon was an effective shield against rioters and hundreds of vehicles underwent the upgrade. The Vehicle Protection Kit (VPK) included ballistic-protection panels for the doors, sills, and bonnet. In addition, an armoured shield for the windscreen had wire-mesh screens

over the windows and lights. Two doors were fitted at the rear and a two-man hatch was installed in the roof. But Makrolon was no protection against blast bombs and high-velocity rounds, which passed straight through.

By the 1980s, the Armoured Protected Vehicle (APV) was introduced. It was a fully protected Land Rover with almost four tonnes of armour to shield passengers and a V8 engine. It quickly became the vehicle of choice for those units serving in Belfast and Londonderry. Based on the strengthened Defender 110 Land Rover chassis, the APV was developed by Glover Webb and was regarded by the military as the 'go to' protected vehicle. The APV could withstand most blasts and high-velocity rounds, although the ❯❯

ABOVE: By the 1980s, the British Army introduced the Armoured Protected Vehicle (APV). It was a fully protected Land Rover with almost four tonnes of armour shielding passengers. DPL

BELOW: A 'bespoke' vehicle later emerged as the 'Snatch' Land Rover. DPL

soldier who stood in the rear, known as 'top cover', remained vulnerable. In the busy streets of West Belfast, the weight of the APV put additional pressure on the brakes and gearbox. In response, a decision was made to develop a 'bespoke' vehicle, which later emerged as the 'Snatch' Land Rover. It included a composite glass fibre armour body and was listed as being capable of stopping high-velocity bullets. At the time of its introduction, violence had reduced in Northern Ireland and by 2003 the 'Snatch' Land Rover was deployed to Iraq. Here the vehicle fell victim to insurgent weapons and was quickly dubbed the 'wheeled coffin'.

Countering the IED

Improvised Explosive Devices had been used in Northern Ireland and were adopted by the Iranian Revolutionary Guard (IRG) in the country's war with Iraq. As Western forces moved into the Middle East, Teheran was quick to supply and train insurgents. When Coalition forces led the intervention into Afghanistan, they had a limited force of protected combat vehicles capable of defeating explosive attacks. Advanced forces entering the north of the country operated on horseback and used procured Toyotas, but in the busy streets of Kabul it was soon evident that protected platforms would be needed – they faced IED attacks from a hardcore of Taliban fighters still at large in the capital. The French government flew in the VAB, a small, armoured personnel carrier, while Italian forces mounted patrols in the Iveco light armoured

platform. The US had a small force in the city and used the Humvee, which offered little cover against roadside bombs. The British used soft-skinned vehicles, mainly the Land Rover, with no protection and highly exposed. Within months, a British soldier was killed when a suicide bomber attacked a patrol in the city. UK politicians demanded extra protection, resulting in the eventual deployment of the Saxon combat vehicle to Kabul. Then, as the operation in Afghanistan continued, the US headed a new intervention in Iraq in 2003 and the number of IED attacks literally exploded on the streets of Baghdad. The American force was initially reliant on its

unprotected Humvee and a small number of LAV wheeled personnel carriers. The roadside bomb attacks soared as insurgents looted stockpiles of explosives and ammunition abandoned by Saddam's army – the Coalition did not have enough soldiers for protection.

By late 2003, insurgents in Iraq were mounting attacks daily, putting pressure on US commanders to improve protection. The US Army's Humvee underwent an immediate amour upgrade, called the Armour Survivability Kit (ASK). It was introduced in October 2003 and added about 1,000lbs to the weight of the vehicle. The war in Afghanistan had continued and by 2006 increased

ABOVE: US Humvee and the British Snatch Land Rover were being destroyed by roadside bombs, so plans were made for a new, enhanced series of protected combat vehicles. US DoD

BELOW: The French government flew in the VAB to Kabul to counter IEDs, while Italian forces mounted patrols in the Iveco light armoured platform. DPL

attacks by insurgents on Coalition forces in Afghanistan had also spiked. US Humvees and the British Snatch Land Rovers were being destroyed by roadside bombs and plans were now under way for a new enhanced series of protected combat vehicles. An improved armour package for the Humvee called the Fragmentation Kit 5 was added. The 'Frag 5' upgrade added additional plating of homogeneous steel armour to the four doors, each weighing 600lbs. A large, armoured cupola fitted to protect the gunner from attack plus armoured plates under the chassis were seen as too much for any IED.

The increased weight initially caused a series of teething problems, which were ironed out in a follow-up review. Most up-armoured variants held up well against attacks, but as the armour increased the insurgents used bigger roadside bombs. By now, a new range of vehicles known as MRAPs (Mine Resistant Ambush Protected) was being built in the United States to counter the impact of the IED. They included the Cougar, which started to arrive in 2007, with other platforms such as the Caiman and the RG-33 – the latter being a South African platform – based on a 1970s design.

As the number of roadside bombs rose, the UK purchased several platforms to replace the Snatch Land Rover and the BV206 (Viking), which were deployed in Iraq and Afghanistan. The US 6x6 Cougar was renamed Mastiff and the 4x4 Cougar was called Ridgback.

These vehicles delivered a step-change in improved protection and were popular with soldiers… but they were heavy and sacrificed speed and manoeuvrability – rendering the vehicle safe, but slow. They had air-conditioning units, NBC overpressure and filter protection, and an electrically powered winch, capable of hauling a four-ton capacity. The Cougar (Mastiff) was produced with run-flat tyre inserts, could operate across undulating terrain and be transported by C-17. Most importantly, the Cougar-H armour kit offered complete all-round protection against 7.62mm rounds, including the windows.

During trials, a 20lb bomb was put between the front and rear axles and a 15lb charge placed under the centre of the chassis. It was detonated and caused little damage to the vehicle. The radiator, tyres, battery compartment, gasoline tanks, engine and gearbox are all covered by ballistic protection. The V-shaped hull's purpose is to deflect the blast outside and away from the passenger cabin. While roadside bombs – depending on their size – may render the vehicle unusable, the test concluded that the occupants would not be hurt.

Although the focus was on protected vehicles, the demand »

BOTTOM: The UK government procured the heavy armoured Cougar from the United States and renamed it the Mastiff. DPL

BELOW: The WMIK, which had been introduced into service in the late 1990s, was first deployed to Sierra Leone and later Afghanistan and Iraq... but it had no armour and was vulnerable to IED attacks. UK MoD

ABOVE: The Ridgback was another successful acquisition from the US family of mine-resistant vehicles. DPL

BELOW: A US Marine Cougar – one of the first MRAP platforms to be deployed to Iraq and Afghanistan. USMC

for small air-portable vehicles for special operations and high-readiness units was also under way. One of these vehicles was the Polaris M-RZR, a new light tactical vehicle (LTV) that delivered off-road manoeuvrability and performance. The Polaris – in two and four-person variants – could be transferred by helicopter and transport aircraft, had a low profile, was fast and easy to maintain. The new vehicle was totally different in design from the standard Land Rover and Humvee platforms, with doors and only tubular framework around the occupants.

British commanders still saw the need for a robust weapons platform that could offer protection from roadside blasts while also being deployed as an open top 'strike platform'. This new vehicle was named the Jackal, also known as MWIK (Mobility Weapon Mounted Installation Kit) and its primary role was to support patrol operations and carry out deep battlespace reconnaissance, rapid assault, and fire support. An updated version of the Jackal was ordered with the crew increased to four and the main armament gun ring moved forward to give it an all-round arc of fire. The chassis was also upgraded, allowing the vehicle to carry a greater payload and additional side armour. A six-wheeled variant of the Jackal, called the Coyote, was produced as a combat carrier and, in 2025, these vehicles were deployed to Eastern Europe to support NATO exercises. The Coyote tactical support vehicle is a larger derivative of the Jackal,

and the two vehicles are designed to work alongside each other.

The UK also developed a series of protected patrol vehicles, named the Foxhound, Husky and Panther. The Foxhound, also known as Ocelot, is a protected patrol vehicle that includes a high level of blast protection for its size and weight. Its design embraced the MRAP capabilities of a V-shaped hull and survived numerous IED attacks in Afghanistan. The second platform, the Husky, was delivered as part of the British Army's protected support vehicle plan, providing a highly mobile and flexible load-carrying vehicle. It has been designed in the United States by Navistar and called the MXT-MV. The British deployed it to Afghanistan where it served on a range of missions and proved highly effective against IEDs. The third platform, the Panther, built by Iveco in Italy, was also ordered. Weighing seven tonnes, it was – like the Foxhound and Husky – air transportable by C-17 and could be underslung beneath a Chinook helicopter. It provided armoured

ABOVE: With a protected, heavy machine gun platform, the Ridgback was regarded as 'bullet proof' by soldiers. UK MoD

ABOVE RIGHT: The Polaris – in two and four-person variants – could be transported by helicopter and transport aircraft. It had a low profile, was fast and easy to maintain. US DoD

RIGHT: The UK also developed a series of protected patrol vehicles – the Foxhound and the Husky and a further upgrade to the Land Rover. UK MoD

protection for four to six soldiers armed and was fitted with a 7.62mm L7 general purpose machine gun. More than 300 were ordered in a £160 million contract that was designed to provide a replacement for the Saxon, the 432 armoured patrol carrier and the Land Rover.

The Panther was planned to become the British Army's Future Command and Liaison Vehicle (FCLV), but in 2018 the entire fleet was put up for sale. Other innovations by the UK military in southern Afghanistan included the Warthog armoured tracked vehicle, a modified and better protected version of the Singapore Industries company Bronco platform. It was equipped with an upgraded cooling and filtration system

and could carry the Bowman communications system. It was protected against IEDs, mines and rocket propelled grenades (RPGs). Warthogs were equipped with a crew-served weapon system that was fitted on top of the vehicle and a protected shield. According to official records, the UK's fleet of 115 Warthogs survived more than 30 direct IED strikes with no crew fatalities: the relatively low strike rate partially attributable to the design's ability to traverse terrain inaccessible to other wheeled or tracked vehicles. In December 2010, a British Army soldier, Lance Corporal William Reeks, survived an IED attack after the Warthog he was travelling in set off an explosive device.

Lesson Learned

Conflict in the Middle East forced a change in the shape of protected vehicles. Mines and explosive devices are hardly new to warfare and were used on a huge scale in World War Two, but when Coalition forces invaded Iraq in 2003 the concept of being attacked with IEDs on a daily basis had not been considered in the pre-deployment planning. The new MRAP platforms – Cougar and Mastiff, often called 'muscle wagons' – were designed to allow occupants to survive a rocket-propelled grenade, a pipe bomb, a car bomb, or any form of IED.

The first MRAPs arrived in Iraq and Afghanistan in 2007. As the war ended, the experience of operations in Afghanistan provided the data for engineers to shape the next generation of combat vehicles that commanders sought as forces returned to contingency operations – conventional warfare. The US military began procuring a new range of light and protected platforms, although super-large platforms used in Helmand, Afghanistan, are regarded as anomalies among modern combat vehicles. Instead, designers have focused on shape and technology, with newer platforms being smaller or bearing a low-profile shape.

In January 2014, the US Army issued a notice to industry for a commercial, off-the-shelf, air-droppable Ultra-Light Combat Vehicle (ULCV), which resulted »

In 2020, the M1301 Infantry Squad Vehicle (ISV), an air-transportable high-speed, light utility vehicle was selected by the United States Army. Based on the Chevrolet Colorado ZR2 platform, it also held nine infantrymen. More than 650 ISVs are being allocated to 11 infantry brigade combat teams (IBCTs) by 2025.

Following the withdrawal from Afghanistan in 2021, the US procured a new all-terrain vehicle called the Joint Light Tactical Vehicle (JLTV), which includes a remote-control weapon system. The idea for this first emerged in 2006 as US forces in Iraq faced an onslaught of IED attacks. Three years later, the Oshkosh all-terrain platform entered service with US forces. It was part of the MRAP family of vehicles and was initially intended to replace the Humvee.

Since its first production, the MRAP All-Terrain Vehicle (M-ATV)

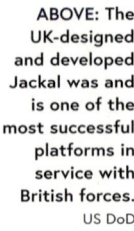

ABOVE: The UK-designed and developed Jackal was and is one of the most successful platforms in service with British forces. US DoD

RIGHT: The Warthog, introduced to replace the BV tracked vehicles in Afghanistan, was fitted with a V-shaped hull. DPL

in the purchase of the Ground Mobility Vehicle (GMV) for the US airborne. Capable of carrying nine soldiers, it can be airlifted by Chinook or Black Hawk. In the same year, the highly mobile Dagor (Deployable Advanced Ground Off Road) platform was ordered. The vehicle is certified for airdrop and internal air transport by CH-47 Chinook heavy-lift helicopters and can be sling-loaded under UH-60 Black Hawk helicopters. The Dagor was developed under contract for the US Special Operations Command (USSOC) and, again, can accommodate up to nine soldiers with four in the cabin, four in the bed

(rear section) and a roof gunner who has a seat suspended from the roll cage in the cabin.

By November 2016, the US Marine Corps (USMC) had signed a $6.5 million contract with Polaris for a number of MRZR-D ATVs. Called the Utility Task Vehicle (UTV), it is a version of the vehicle already in use by the USSOC but is designed to be diesel-powered. The USMC bought the unarmoured ATVs because they can fit inside an MV-22 Osprey, enabling them to be deployed at long distances, to provide logistics support to ground combat units. The vehicles can carry four troops and have a small cargo bed capable of carrying 1,500lbs of payload.

has undergone several upgrades. In May 2015, Oshkosh announced it had secured a contract with the US Army to upgrade 360 M-ATVs. Two years later in January 2017, the US Marine Corps disclosed that they would upgrade and refurbish 80 of their M-ATVs.

The M-ATV proved to be more survivable than the Humvee and was lighter than other MRAP versions, but to further enhance survivability and mobility for troops, the US military undertook the Joint Light Tactical Vehicle (JLTV) project to obtain a vehicle combining light weight, mobility, and protection. The JLTV also produced by Oshkosh is a light utility/combat multi-role vehicle. But while the majority of 'light' vehicles offer little protection the JLTV was enclosed and again listed as a replacement for the Humvee.

ABOVE: Despite a successful period of service in Afghanistan, the Warthog was later retired by the UK. DPL

LEFT: The JLTV is seen as one of the US military's most advanced protected vehicles. US DoD

BELOW: In January 2014, a notice to industry was issued for a commercial, off-the-shelf, air-droppable Ultra-Light Combat Vehicle (ULCV), which resulted in the purchase of the Ground Mobility Vehicle. US MoD

Chapter Four

NATO – OPERATIONS IN THE HIGH NORTH AND EUROPE

RIGHT: Many NATO nations operate variants of the Bv 206 or 410 tracked vehicles. Norwegian MoD

NATO nations have followed the principal of fielding both light 'unarmoured' and 'protected' vehicles. The southern European countryside is renowned for its flat open terrain which saw the deployment of tank brigades during the tense years of the Cold War between Moscow and the West. Today, the Alliance also faces security issues in the High North where tracked platforms are the most suited vehicle to cope with the arduous conditions of the Arctic snow and ice. Here Russia is the primary adversary, and protected vehicles don't just protect soldiers from the enemy, they can also be a shelter from the killer weather. When fighting and operating in such hostile conditions, the value of protected mobility is the difference between life and death. Eastern Europe and the Baltic States are also areas of concern where advanced protected mobility is critical. In

BELOW: The Bv 410 is the most advanced of the tracked family of vehicles which have proved so successful. UK MoD

Latvia, Estonia and Lithuania the Alliance has deployed troops on a mission codenamed Operation Enhanced Forward Presence, amid the political concern of an incursion by Moscow. Here nations have deployed their latest platforms.

High North

The High North is strategically important to the Alliance as it presents an obvious gateway for Russian forces to assault through the Finland gap and sweep into Sweden, Norway and Denmark.

ABOVE: In the frozen wasteland of the High North, tracked combat vehicles are the most effective, with wheeled platforms operating at lower altitude on harden roads. UK MoD

RIGHT: NATO faces security issues in the High North where tracked platforms are the most suited vehicle to meet the challenges of the Arctic's snow and ice. UK MoD

platform used by many NATO nations with numerous variants and models in service. This tracked articulated all terrain carrier was first developed by Sweden's Hägglund & Söner and subsequently BAE Systems. It consists of two units, with all four tracks being powered. It can carry up to 17 soldiers – six in the front compartment and 11 in the rear. Colloquially known as the BV, it is fitted with a small amount of armour and can be airlifted by support helicopters. The standard Bv 206 engine is quiet and hard to hear on the ice-packed slopes where its engine sound is often shielded by the windy conditions. Finland »

This area's importance has earned it special significance with the Alliance headquarters which lists the region as 'the Northern flank'. Finland and Sweden's recent accession to NATO has reinforced Northern Europe's security, as the two countries bridge what was an obvious entry point in the alliance's territory between Norway in the Arctic, and Estonia, Latvia, and Lithuania in the Baltic Sea. To deter any attempt by Moscow to assault through the northern flank, the Alliance carries out annual winter exercises to test readiness and equipment in the harsh conditions of the Arctic tundra. Here in the frozen wasteland tracked combat vehicles are the most effective, with wheeled platforms operating at lower altitude on hard roads.

The tracked Bandvagn 206 (Bv 206) combat vehicle is a universal

RIGHT: The Finns also operate the Sisu, a Finnish produced four-wheel drive mine-resistant ambush protected vehicle. Finnish MoD

RIGHT: The UK Commando Force have also procured snowmobiles, officially called the Lynx Brutal Over Snow Reconnaissance Vehicles, which are due to be delivered in late 2025. UK MoD

BELOW: Norway also used the six-wheel Coyote which can carry a large volume of supplies to support frontline troops. UK MoD

operates a similar tracked all-terrain vehicle called the Nasu, meaning Piglet. It looks like an earlier version of the Bv 206, but it is an entirely new design. Almost 1m longer and 2,205lb heavier, it has bigger payload-carrying capability than the Bv 206. The low ground pressure enables the Nasu to cope with a wide range of difficult conditions. It is also fully amphibious, with a speed in water of up to 6kts. The Finns also operate the Sisu, a Finnish-produced four-wheel drive mine-resistant ambush-protected vehicle which sits high off the ground and can carry six soldiers. It replaced the South African RG-32M and can operate in the air-defence, command and control, as well as medical roles.

Norwegian forces are a key user of the BV and operates wheeled vehicles too. The Italian Iveco, a Light Multirole Vehicle (LMV) can be fitted with modular armour packs to adjust its level of protection to meet the mission requirement.

ABOVE: To deter any attempt by Moscow to assault through the northern flank, the Alliance carries out annual winter exercises to test readiness and equipment in the harsh conditions of the Arctic tundra. US DoD

LEFT: The M301 Infantry Squad Vehicle (ISV) heads the country's light role platform. US DoD

The vehicle's ground clearance has been increased to 19.4in without increasing the overall height. It also uses suspended seats of aeronautical design, a V-shaped under body, and a collapsible sandwich structure in

the floor to deflect and absorb mine blasts. Mobility is helped by a run-flat system, allowing the vehicle to move even with completely deflated tyres. Norway also operates the British six-wheeled High Mobility Transporter. It first entered service in Afghanistan in 2007, and while it has a high wheelbase and armoured side panels, the cabin section is open, giving the crew a 360° visibility. Finnish special operations forces operate the Polaris MV7 six-wheeled all-terrain vehicles. This light platform is mainly used by two soldiers and has a rear cargo space.

The Swedish military also operate the BV, using the more specialist Bv 410 model – an ungraded variant of earlier BVs. It was designed »

LEFT: Norwegian forces are a key user of the BV and also operate several wheeled platforms including the Italian Iveco, a Light Multirole Vehicle (LMV) which can be fitted with modular armour packs to adjust its level of protection. US DoD

for the UK Royal Marines and is a tracked articulated amphibious all-terrain armoured vehicle produced by BAE Systems Hägglunds of Sweden. The 410 has a small front to it, while the 206 is flat fronted. The northern European nation also operates the five-seat South African wheeled RG-32 Scout, used by the Finnish military. It provides protection against small arms fire, grenades and roadside bombs. Denmark's special operations Jaeger Corps operate the Supacat 4x4, while the infantry use the Mowag Eagle which offers protected mobility. Produced by General Dynamics, this armoured platform can carry five personnel and operates a remote-controlled weapon system.

Both the Royal Marines and USMC have trained in the High North since the 1960s to maintain NATO's high readiness in the region. The UK first adopted the Bv 202, which offered an all-terrain capability and a manual gearbox which many drivers regarded as quieter than the modern automatic transmission. Today, the Bv 410, known as the Viking, is the first choice for the UK Commando Force. It is the perfect platform for operations in the Arctic as it is tracked, armoured and amphibious. The Bv 410 has a more powerful Cummins 5.9litre diesel engine than the Bv 206, as well as

improved ground clearance and an upgraded chassis. A small number of Vikings, fitted with slay armour, were deployed to Afghanistan at the end of summer 2006 but proved vulnerable to Improvised Explosive Devices (IEDs).

The Royal Marines use quad bikes to give them the edge in combat. Small, lightweight and agile, these vehicles allow mortars and their crews to be moved rapidly around the battlefield, avoiding detection. The Can-Am six-wheel quad bikes used by the Royal Marines feature a 38hp single-cylinder

Rotax 427 engine to enable them to descend on the enemy quickly. They can be fitted with tracks to cope with harsher conditions. The UK Commando Force have also procured snowmobiles, called the Lynx Brutal Over Snow Reconnaissance Vehicles (Lynx Brutal OSRV), which are due to be delivered in late 2025. These platforms have been trialled in Norway and will allow the commandos to strike faster and further across the Arctic region. Made by Finnish subsidiary of Canadian firm Bombardier, the Lynx Brutal is

ABOVE: The Canadians also field the Polaris light vehicle, seen here leaving a transport plane. Canadian MoD

BELOW: The United States, the powerhouse of military vehicle design, continues to evolve a range of combat vehicles. UD DoD

custom-built to operate in deep snow and is ideally suited for taking troops and their equipment deep into the battlespace, giving them the tactical advantage.

North America and UK

Canada's military has invested in a range of 'light and protected' vehicles to fulfil the country's defence policy and its commitment to NATO. Like many military formations in the Alliance, the Canadians operate a number of BVs to support operations in areas such as Ellesmore and Nunavut in the north of the country as well as NATO's High North. The M301 Infantry Squad Vehicle (ISV) heads the country's light role platform. Made in the United States, this air-portable nine-man vehicle entered service in late 2024 and is deployed with the Canadian Brigade deployed in Latvia. The »

ABOVE: The Cougar, MaxxPro, Caiman and Oshkosh M-ATV were all deployed in Afghanistan.
US Marines

RIGHT: The Army M1297 Army Ground Mobility Vehicle (AGMV) has been introduced with airborne forces. US DoD

BELOW: The MaxxPro MRAP is one of the protected vehicles deployed by Canada. US DoD

ABOVE: Variants of the Land Rover are still in use by UK advance forces with the Weapons Mounted Installation Kit (WMIK) and Revised WMIK. UK MoD

BELOW: The UK operates the Foxhound, a protected four-wheel drive vehicle, which was introduced in 2008 and can carry four soldiers in the rear and two in the front. UK MoD

M301 is an air-transportable high-speed, light utility vehicle powered by a Duramax 2.8L turbo-charged diesel engine connected to a Hydro-Matic 6-speed automatic transmission. It is a doorless design, with steel and aluminium body panels, has disc brakes and a run-flat insert. The M301 is supported by the Dagor and MRZR-D Polaris vehicles, both produced in the US. The Canadian military's protected platforms are focussed on the heavily armoured Cougar which was deployed to Afghanistan.

The United States, the powerhouse of military vehicle design, continues to evolve a range of combat vehicles. Many of these heavy Mine-Resistant Ambush Protected (MRAP)

platforms, which were first deployed in Iraq and Afghanistan, are held in readiness for future conflicts. The Cougar, MaxxPro, Caiman and Oshkosh M-ATV powerful protected vehicles can withstand most medium-range mine, roadside bombs and rocket propelled grenades. Meanwhile, the Humvee has been at the centre of several plans to replace it, but the four-wheel drive vehicle remains in service, albeit with limited units of the US military.

US Special Operations units have invested in the M1297 Army Ground Mobility Vehicle (AGMV), a small lightweight jeep which can carry nine soldiers and their equipment. They also operate the Dagor, which again can carry nine and like the AGMV can be helicopter-borne into the battlefield or

dropped by parachute. The Pentagon also maintains a small fleet of fast interceptors which can operate on long range patrols and be re-supplied by air. They include the advanced light strike vehicle, the Interim Fast Attack Vehicle, the Desert Patrol vehicle and the M1161 – all have been designed to reduce the vehicle's profile, are manned with a two or three crew and are fitted with heavy machine guns. The US also operates the tracked BV vehicles in support of their cold weather warfare commitments.

Meanwhile, Britain is replacing the heavy protected Mastiff family of vehicles with the Boxer mechanised infantry vehicles in 2030. The Boxer is an eight-wheeled multirole vehicle produced by Rheinmetall and part of a family of combat vehicles designed

by an international consortium. Fitted with a Rolls-Royce multifuel engine and automatic transmission, the UK order will focus on the personnel carrier variant. It bears a unique module design consisting of a drive module and a mission module. it can be rapidly adapted to suit various military missions, roles and scenarios. To reduce thermal signature, the Boxer's hot exhaust is discharged together with the cooling air via thermally insulated ducts.

The UK also operates the Foxhound, a protected four-wheel drive vehicle, which was introduced in 2008 and can carry four soldiers in the rear and two in the front. The modular design means that any blast-damaged components can also be easily and quickly replaced

in the field. The four-wheel Jackal and six-wheel Coyote have armoured protection to the side but offer little protection for the crew who sit on an open platform. Both are used by the infantry for reconnaissance and are supported by the small Polaris light platforms which the Royal Marines and Ranger Regiments operate. Variants of the Land Rover are still in use by UK advance forces with the Weapons Mounted Installation Kit (WMIK) and Revised WMIK both able to be lifted by helicopter and air transport planes. A potential replacement for the Land Rover is a militarised version of the Toyota Land Cruiser 70 being developed by Babcock Defence.

Europe

Many European nations operate generic light and protected vehicles that are proven in conflict and meet the NATO operational standard for vehicles. In Belgium the country's Para-commando units operate the light Jankel Wolf. This is based on the Unimog U5000 platform and has little

protection. It is supported by the Jankel Fox rapid response vehicle, and both have a reputation for good reliability. Again, this vehicle is based on the Toyota Land Cruiser and although it can be fitted with side armour, it has no overhead protection. A 360° machine gun mount ring is fitted in the rear which can also accommodate a grenade launcher. Belgium also operates the protected Iveco multi-role vehicle, used by Norway, Spain and Italy. In addition, Brussels has procured the US produced Joint Light Tactical Vehicle (JLTV) which sits high off the ground, is mine resistant and used by the US Army.

France has some of the most advanced vehicles in NATO with their special operations group operating the Panhard VPS, a light 4x4 patrol vehicle especially designed for the country's Special Forces. The Panhard VPS (Véhicule Patrouille Spéciale) was selected by the French Army to meet a requirement for a light, rapidly deployable vehicle capable of long-duration missions in extremes of »

LEFT: In Belgium the country's Para-Commando units operate the light Jankel 'Wolf'. It is based on the Unimog U5000 platform but has little protection. Belgium Army

BOTTOM: France has some of the most advanced vehicles in NATO with their special operations group operating the Panhard VPS, a light 4x4 patrol vehicle especially designed for the country's Special Forces. Bob Morrison/DPL

BELOW: Belgium also operates the protected vehicles Iveco light multi-role vehicle, also used by Norway, Spain and Italy. NATO

climate. The VPS has an extended range for long patrols and features an armoured floor which provides blast protection to the crew against mines and IEDs. It has a payload of 2,600lb so it can perform a wide variety of missions and is air-transportable by C-160 Transall or C-130 Hercules. France also operates the Rider, a small two-man buggy which is air-transportable by helicopter and transport planes. It can carry anti-tank weapons and, if needed, can tow a small trailer. A veteran vehicle called the VLRA ((Véhicule de Liaison, de Reconnaissance et d'Appui), first used in 1969 by the French as a reconnaissance platform, is still in service. This iconic platform sits high off the ground and is known for its reliability, simplicity, ruggedness and the commonality of its vehicle parts across the globe. According to Jane's *Defence Review*, the UK ordered 20 in 1996.

Paris also operates the VBL (Véhicule Blindé Léger) and PVP (Petit Véhicule Protégé) small, armoured combat vehicles. First introduced in the 1980s, it is fully amphibious with a small propellor fitted below the rear step, and it can be transported by the C-130, C-160 and A400M aircraft. The VBL has been used in many peacekeeping operations of the French Army, notably in Lebanon, Bosnia, Rwanda and Kosovo. The PVP light protected vehicle is a general-purpose armoured four-wheel drive vehicle made by Panhard. The French military is also introducing new protected platforms with the VBMRT – L Serval (Véhicule Blindé Multi-Rôle

Léger Serval), an armoured protected platform designed to replace the iconic VAB (Véhicule de l'Avant Blindé) which has been in service for decades. The Serval is designed to provide protection for troops in close contact with the enemy. It is highly manoeuvrable and will be assigned to 11th Airborne and the 27th Mountain Infantry Brigades.

The Italian Army operates the British Land Rover (WMIK) and Aris Light Tactical Assault vehicle for its special forces. The US produced Ground Mobility Vehicle is also in service with Italy's airborne forces as a light strike vehicle. The Iveco light multirole vehicle (LMV) is in service as a protected platform. It uses modular armour packs to adjust

ABOVE: Paris operates the VBL and PVP small, armoured combat vehicles. The VBL has been used in many French Army peacekeeping operations, notably in Lebanon, Bosnia, Rwanda and Kosovo. Ministère des Armées

LEFT: The French military is also introducing new protected platforms with the VBMRT – L Serval (Véhicule Blindé Multi-Rôle Léger Serval), an armoured protected platform designed to replace the iconic VAB which has been in service for decades. Ministère des Armées

is also used by the Dutch special operations group. This is an 8-tonne vehicle designed to replace the Landsysteme Light Infantry Support Vehicle, known as the Serval. Powered by a multifuel six-cylinder diesel engine, Vector has a turning circle of 6ft and a maximum speed of 70mph. Additionally, the vehicle is capable of being air transported by C130, A400, C17 transport aircraft and the CH47 helicopter.

German forces use the US produced Polaris MRZR-D for advanced force

operations and the LAPVG Enok, a four-wheel protected patrol vehicle which entered service in 2008 for use by the country's Kommando Spezialkrafte. It can carry six people and is designed to offer protection against small arms fire, land mines and IEDs. The military's protected vehicles include the Mowag Eagle, an MRAP designed vehicle which was produced by the Swiss. The first Eagles used the chassis and running gear of the Humvee which entered service in 2003. It was developed for the needs ››

BELOW: Sweden's protected vehicles include the Eagle, an MRAP designed vehicle which was designed by the Swiss company Mowag. MoD Sweden

its level of protection to its mission requirements and is also in service with Belgium, Norway and Spain.

The German Bundeswehr has procured the Dutch-developed Defenture, listed as the Versatile Expeditionary Commando Tactical Off-Road Vehicle (Vector), which

LEFT: The German Bundeswehr has procured the Dutch developed Defenture Vector, which is also used by the Dutch special operations group. Federal MoD

LEFT: One of the most specialist vehicles operated by any European force is the Polish PWA Aero, an off-road vehicle designed for airborne units. It can carry two soldiers and is adapted to be dropped by parachute.
MoD Poland

of the Swiss Army and is also operated by Denmark and Luxembourg. A development plan is currently underway to replace the vehicle.

The Fennek, a low-profile Light Armoured four-wheeled armed reconnaissance vehicle produced by German company KNDS and Dutch Defence Vehicle Systems, is in service with Sweden, Germany and Holland. This small, protected platform was deployed in Afghanistan by Germany and the Netherlands. In 2007, a Dutch Fennek was hit by an IED which killed one soldier and wounded two other occupants. The vehicle and its crew were taking part in an offensive operation targeting the Taliban in the province of Uruzgan, Afghanistan. In another incident, a German Fennek was hit by a rocket-propelled grenade. Its hollow charge jet penetrated the vehicle through the right front wheel rim, passed through the vehicle and blew the left door off its hinge.

LEFT: The Polish Army is undergoing a major investment to replace its legacy Soviet platforms with a new fleet of combat vehicles.
MoD Poland

BELOW: The Fennek, a low-profile Light Armoured four-wheeled armed reconnaissance vehicle produced by German company KNDS and Dutch Defence Vehicle Systems, is in service with Sweden, Germany and Holland.
Federal MoD

Germany and the Netherlands pioneered the introduction of the new Boxer – an eight-wheeled protected platform which the UK has also purchased. Lithuania has also elected to field the vehicle.

The Polish Army is undergoing a major investment to replace its legacy

Soviet platforms with a new fleet of combat vehicles. Its light products include the Honker Skorpion-3 and ZWD-3, both light all-terrain vehicles used by the country's special forces. They were deployed in Iraq and plans are underway to replace them.

One of the most specialist vehicles operated by any European force is the Polish PWA Aero, an off-road vehicle designed for airborne units. It can carry two soldiers and is adapted to be dropped by parachute. Poland's protected vehicles include the KTO Rosomak, known as the Wolverine. This eight-wheel multi-role military vehicle is a Finnish design produced under licence in Poland. Poland deployed 100 KTO Rosomak vehicles, which were fitted with additional armour, to Afghanistan. The Rosomak upgraded armour was able to defeat rocket-propelled grenades and survived several attacks in 2008.

Spain has developed the Vamtac multi-purpose armoured patrol vehicle to meet the requirements of the military for a multipurpose, air-portable, high mobility off-road vehicle. In service since the early 2000s, the vehicle is powered by a six-cylinder diesel engine with a protected cabin and an open cargo deck in the rear. It has been deployed on operations in Afghanistan, the Congo and Lebanon.

Spain also operates the Italian Iveco LMV and the South African RG-31 – both mine protected and highly mobile vehicles. Finally, Portugal also operates the Vamtac.

Eastern Europe

The war in Ukraine has seen NATO nations send hundreds of combat

vehicles to support Kyiv's forces. These 'gifted' vehicles range from light strike platforms to heavily protected vehicles, many of which have been fitted with drone defence 'cages' on the top of the vehicles and additional side protection to counter rocket-propelled grenades.

Latvia, Estonia and Lithuania operate the Humvee, the Land Rover and the Mercedes G Wagon which form the country's light vehicle capability. The Finnish Patria six-wheeled armoured combat vehicle heads the protected platforms. It can carry ten soldiers and is also in service with Sweden and is being reviewed by Germany. Estonia has procured the Nurol Yörük light armoured infantry vehicle and the Otokat Arma six-wheeled armoured protected platform from Turkey. In total, Turkey will supply 240 vehicles which are scheduled to be delivered by late 2025. Lithuania has ordered 500 variants of the US Joint Light Tactical Vehicle (JLTV).

ABOVE: In eastern Europe the IAG Guardian produced in the United Arab Emirates is fielded by Hungary. UAE Defence

TOP: Spain has developed the Vamtac armoured patrol vehicle to meet the requirements of the military for a multipurpose, air-portable, high mobility off-road vehicle. Spain MoD

LEFT: Estonia has procured the Nurol Yörük light armoured infantry vehicle and the Otokat Arma six-wheeled armoured protected platform from Turkey. MoD Turkey

Chapter Five

STRIKE VEHICLES
FOR HIGH-READINESS OPERATIONS

LEFT: Special operations forces, such as forward operations groups, need lightweight, fast vehicles that can be airlifted by helicopter or dropped by parachute into remote areas, ready to operate over rugged terrain. UK MoD

Advanced forces, such as special operations groups, need lightweight, fast vehicles that can be airlifted by helicopter, dropped by parachute into remote areas and are able to operate in the most rugged terrain. These platforms rarely have any armoured protection – their sole objective is to sustain the crew in hostile environments in order that they can achieve their objective.

They must be able to wade through rivers or operate in soft sand, in the Arctic or in open countryside of eastern Europe and beyond.

In the post-war years, the British Land Rover was the 'go to' vehicle and remains a favourite with many forces. But since the 1991 Gulf War, a new range of platforms often referred to as 'strike vehicles' has emerged to compete with the Land Rover. These low-profile innovations were used by

US and British forces in the war, with the American 'Chenowth' making its first appearance. The British alternative was made by the Longline company and was built for hit-and-run missions. By the mid-1990s, the vehicle was adopted by the UK's newly formed 24th Airmobile Brigade and served for several years before being retired. Those who used it said it was highly reliable, easy to maintain and could operate in most conditions.

BELOW: The size of these vehicles allowed the team to carry enough stores to deploy for weeks and units often carried small motorbikes fitted to the rear for close reconnaissance. Australian MoD

Strike vehicles

The changing shape of warfare has created new demands from special operations units who need to be able to operate for longer periods in the field, carrying more weapons systems as well as ammunition, fuel, and rations to sustain extended patrols. The concept of long patrols was pioneered in the North African desert in the 1940s and later adopted by many armies.

When the Australian military needed to maintain a presence across the country's northern territories with long patrols, Land Rover developed the six-wheel Patrol Vehicle (PV) to operate in these remote areas. It was used by the Australian Special Air Service with the first ones being modified Series II Land Rovers that were developed in the 1970s. The larger, six-wheel modified variant followed and was called the Long-Range Patrol Vehicle (LRPV). It was developed in the late 1980s and designed to be mechanically simple and easy to maintain. It was fitted with a central ring-mount for a heavy machine gun or grenade launcher, as well as a further gun mount in front of the passenger. The size of these vehicles allowed the team to carry enough stores to deploy for weeks and units often carried small motorbikes fitted to the rear for close reconnaissance. The Australian SAS deployed the LRPV to Bagram air base north of Kabul when Coalition Forces »

ABOVE: The BV tracked 410 might not seem like a strike or assault platform, but in Afghanistan it was used to ferry a commando unit across open ground and a river to attack a Taliban fort. UK MoD

LEFT: The French VPS platform is used by high-readiness forces. Bob Morrison/DPL

LEFT: In the post-war years, the British Land Rover was the 'go to' vehicle and remains a favourite with many forces. DPL

ABOVE: Land Rover developed the six-wheel patrol vehicle to operate in remote areas and was procured for the Australian Special Air Service. DPL

It was a two-person platform, used in the anti-tank (AT) role with Milan AT systems strapped to a small rack above the crew and a 7.62mm machine gun mounted in front of the passenger. The concept saw the LSV operate in groups deployed to ambush tanks, but despite their established role the vehicles were withdrawn from service after five years.

In 1994, Land Rover unveiled the 'Wolf' variant and at the same time the UK automotive company Supacat designed and built an All-Terrain Multi-Purpose (ATMP) platform that was seen as revolutionary. It was small, met all the operational roles of being air-transportable, was fast and could operate in the anti-tank role. It was deployed with British forces in Kosovo and during the withdrawal these small vehicles were able to carry as many as eight soldiers. Steyr Pinzgauer, an Austria-based company, built an all-terrain four-wheel drive that the British Army procured. It was used by the Royal Marines and the Parachute Regiment as a light patrol platform, capable of carrying six soldiers. It was seen as being a strike platform and, if needed, a logistics vehicle.

moved into Afghanistan after 9/11. It was the perfect platform for the remote conditions. Later, it was also sent to Iraq and was able to support extended patrols deep into the western desert.

UK forces have used the Land Rover since the 1950s with the vehicle undergoing numerous upgrades. The Defender variant was procured by the British Army, armed and used across the globe in the 1980s. Earlier, for many years, by removing doors and windows for the 'light role', the Land Rover was used in the desert by special forces for missions in Oman when the vehicle was fitted with machine guns mounted on a raised commander's seat in the late 1950s. A .30 Cal machine gun was fitted facing to the rear and manned by the vehicle's radio operator. A decade later the requirement for a long-range platform resulted in the SAS adopting the Series IIA 90 Land Rover. The larger Series II could carry more stores and support longer-range operations than its predecessor. The SAS painted its Land Rovers a sandy colour that many regarded as being closer to pink – it was found to be excellent camouflage in the desert. In the 1980s, the Land Rover 110 became the platform for the SAS's new Desert Patrol Vehicle (DPV). The DPV had coiled-spring suspension, providing for a much more comfortable ride than its predecessor; it was powered by a 3.5-litre V8 diesel engine.

The work to deliver a bespoke platform suitable for special operations and assault forces continued throughout the 1980s. By the 1990s, the UK and US were developing the first of this new

generation of platforms. The British Army procured the light strike vehicle (LSV) which entered service in 1992 and was designed for fast hit-and-run raids, special operations, and low-intensity guerrilla warfare.

RIGHT: UK forces have used the Land Rover since the 1950s and have benefitted from numerous upgrades. DPL

LEFT: The UK procured the light strike vehicle, which entered service in 1992 and was designed for fast hit-and-run raids, special operations, and low-intensity guerrilla warfare. DPL

BOTTOM: The Russia-produced Tigr that Moscow has allocated for strike operations in Ukraine. DPL

BELOW: The Russians have focused on all-protection vehicles such as the Atlet, which has been deployed in Ukraine. Russian MoD

Prior to the war in Ukraine, the Russian Army invested heavily in strike vehicles for the Spetsnaz forces (special operations). But its doctrine had changed, and it opted to utilise protected vehicles for special operations and infantry with platforms such as the VPK-3927 being rolled out in late 2012. This powerful-looking, fully armoured vehicle, called the Wolf by Russian troops, is capable of withstanding small arms and large IEDs. Putin's forces also operate the AMN- 233121 Atlet and the Tigr – both of them heavily protected, all-terrain platforms. However, they do not appear to have performed well in Ukraine »

and analysts claim these platforms
are not as armoured as Moscow
claims. In October 2024 a new
Russian armoured vehicle, designed
for special operations, appeared
in Ukraine. Called the Sarmat-3,
it is smaller and while it includes
a protected cabin it has an open
storage space at the rear and a heavy
machine gun mount. The vehicle's
fuel range is estimated at 400 miles,
making it ideal for operations in
challenging terrain.

US operations

US special operations forces had,
with few exceptions, relied on
the High Mobility Multipurpose
Wheeled Vehicle (HMMWV;
colloquial: Humvee) for decades: it
was introduced to replace the M151
jeep and entered service in 1985. The
Special Forces operated what they
called the 'War Pig' in Operation
Desert Storm – it was a modified
2.5-ton M1078 lorry that was stripped
bare of doors before having various
mounted weapons systems fitted,
including heavy machine guns and
anti-tank missiles. US commanders
had witnessed the UK Land Rover
in the Gulf War and noted that it
was easier to operate in the desert
terrain that the larger Humvee,
but they still opted to retain the
Humvee. However, the US Rangers,
America's high-readiness troops,
saw the Land Rover as a reliable
replacement for their M151 jeeps
and after consultations the Ranger
Special Operations Vehicle (RSOV)
was developed as a bespoke platform
for the elite US unit. Prototypes used
3.5-litre V8 engines, and final models
used four-cylinder turbo diesel
engines with a manual transmission.
The Rangers operated three main
types of RSOV as weapons, medical

and communications carriers. The weapons vehicle could carry up to 8,000lbs and was designed for a crew of three with additional capacity to ferry as many as seven soldiers in extreme circumstances. In total, 60 vehicles were delivered and first deployed as part of the US security force at the 1992 summer Olympic Games in Spain. New protected vehicles, known as MRAPs (Mine Resistant Ambush Protected), which came into service from 2007 onwards, were not directly suitable for special operations. Instead, US forces used Toyotas and commercial off-the-shelf pick-ups that are readily

ABOVE: The Ranger Special Operations Vehicle (RSOV) was developed as a bespoke platform for the elite US unit. US MoD

LEFT: The US military has introduced the Joint Light Tactical Vehicle (JLTV). US MoD

available in most countries and which they continue to deploy.

Special forces' quest

Building the ultimate light strike vehicle that is air-portable and can support high-readiness units has remained a quest for special operations forces. Within a couple of years of the British Wolf Land Rover being produced, the company unveiled what appeared to be the British Army's first 'technical' vehicle. In conjunction with Ricardo Vehicle Engineering, the Weapons Mounted Installation Kit (WMIK) vehicle was developed – a Land Rover with mounted machine guns, no doors or overhead protection. It featured a strengthened chassis, was fitted with roll cages and a »

LEFT: US special operations in Helmand operated the Ground Mobility Vehicle (GMV). DPL

ABOVE: The Panhard VPS was vulnerable on roads around villages and towns where insurgents planted roadside bombs. Ministère des Armées

ABOVE MIDDLE: The Land Rover RWIMK was used as a patrol, strike, and reconnaissance platform. UK MoD

BELOW: In conjunction with Ricardo Vehicle Engineering, the Weapons Mounted Installation Kit (WMIK) vehicle was a Land Rover with mounted machine guns, no doors or overhead protection. DPL

heavy machine mount in the rear. The first models were deployed to Sierra Leone in 1999 when UK forces were initially sent to West Africa on an evacuation mission as civil war threatened. They later remained in a peace-keeping and advisory role. Then, when UK infantry forces moved into Afghanistan in late 2001 as the first ISAF (International Security and Liaison Force) troops on the ground in Kabul, they deployed a small number of WMIK Land Rovers while US forces relied on Humvees – the Australians were the only force with a dedicated strike vehicle, using their six-wheeled LRPV. The British also used the Pinzgauer in Kabul in a patrol role, while Paris deployed the more protected VAB. Norway and Italy operated the Iveco LMV to ensure a higher level of protection for their troops.

Within a couple of years, the US-led Coalition mounted the 2003 invasion of Iraq and the requirement for both protected and improved strike vehicles was quickly highlighted. French forces, who had also used the VAB in Kabul, moved towards more agile vehicles for their special operations with an upgraded Panhard VPS entering service in 2005. Similar to the WMIK, it featured front and rear machine gun mounts and could be ferried into action by helicopter. In Afghanistan it initially proved a considerable asset in urban areas, but the threat of IEDs reduced its use in built-up areas.

By 2006, the conflict in Afghanistan saw UK forces moving into Helmand in the south of the country. Here the WMIK was a favourite in areas of open terrain, but like the Panhard VPS it was

vulnerable on roads around villages and towns where insurgents planted roadside bombs. To counter this threat, Land Rover upgraded the WMIK to what was listed as the RWIMK (Revised Weapons Mounted Installation Kit). The facelift gave the vehicle armoured side panels, small, armoured doors, and a stores rack above the driver as well as additional electronic counter-measures equipment. The Land Rover RWIMK was used as a patrol, strike, and reconnaissance platform. Manned by a crew of three – commander, driver, and gunner – it could carry a range of weapons including the General-Purpose Machine Gun (GPMG), the Heavy Machine Gun (HMG) and a Grenade Machine Gun (GMG). US special operations in Helmand operated the Ground Mobility Vehicle (GMV). The GMV

a crew of three, was fitted with two-gun mounts and sat high off the ground. Its 5.9-litre Cummins engine was able to deliver speeds up to 70mph depending on the terrain. It was quickly deployed to Helmand and proved a major success – its only downfall being that on occasions when packed with ammunition, food and fuel the vehicle sank in soft sand.

The armour on the Jackal was developed by Jankel Armouring Limited and incorporated armour plating beneath the crew compartment and on the vehicle sides. The Jackal design was unique in that it delivered a strike capability with protection while the crew area was open to the elements. An updated version of the Jackal increased the crew to four. The chassis was upgraded, allowing the vehicle to carry a greater payload, and additional armour against roadside bombs was fitted. It also had a larger 6.7-litre engine. Called the Jackal 2 and known as the Coyote, it was used on sustained desert patrols.

NATO nations were now upgrading their capability with the Italian Aris Light Tactical Assault Vehicle planned to arrive in late 2020, which looks like a Lamborghini and can carry four soldiers as well as the standard gun mounts. By the mid-2020s, the US Army was focusing on light platforms and procured the M1297 Army Ground Mobility Vehicle (A-GMV or AGMV). It could be dropped by parachute, ferried by helicopter, and was

seen as the new vehicle for light infantry brigades. The A-GMV is configured to carry an airborne infantry combat squad of nine paratroopers and their equipment as well as having a payload capacity of more than 5,000lbs. The vehicle has an open design with remote and manned turrets.

Demand continued to develop for a lighter, all-terrain platform and the US special operations procured the Polaris MRZR in 2013. The RZR 800 vehicle was the first variant to enter service and was followed by the Polaris MRZR. The vehicle was adopted by the US Marines and the UK Royal Marines and also the UK Ranger Regiment. Many nations are upgrading and developing platforms for special forces operations. The Spanish army has recently taken delivery of the Neton – a high-tech, all-terrain vehicle based on a Toyota chassis that entered service in 2021. The Neton has seating for four, with a central weapons ring mount and secondary commander's pintle mount. Manufacturer Einsa says additional variants can carry up to eight soldiers. The Neton is air-transportable by C-130 and A400M military aircraft and can be carried inside a CH-47 Chinook helicopter. The delivery of the new platform is a significant boost to special operations capability of the Spanish army.

The French military received its first batch of four Serval (not to be confused with the German patrol vehicle) armoured combat vehicles in 2023 with the remainder due into service by 2030. »

BELOW RIGHT: Developed by the UK-based company Supacat, the Jackal, officially listed as the MWMIK (Mobility Weapon Mounted Installation Kit), had a crew of three, was fitted with two-gun mounts and sat high off the ground. UK MoD

BELOW: In Afghanistan, the WMIK initially proved a considerable asset in urban areas, but the threat of IEDs reduced its use in built-up regions. DPL

(Humvee variant) had a range of 275 miles and a top speed of 60mph. It was specifically designed for operations behind enemy lines and included a hardened cab with an open rear, where an enclosed cabin would normally be. A machine gun mount was fitted in this area, which was also used to store all the fuel, ammunition, rations, repair tools and electronic gadgets. A GMV was designed for a crew of three.

Seeking change

By 2007, the UK Ministry of Defence had rolled out a new platform that combined protection from roadside bombs but was fast and designed to enhance patrol and strike operations. Developed by the UK-based company Supacat, the Jackal – officially listed as the MWMIK (Mobility Weapon Mounted Installation Kit) – had

This platform has been specifically tailored for the requirements of special operations missions. The 4×4 vehicle is combat proven in a variety of challenging climates. The Serval appears on paper to be engineered to the same standard as the Australian Bushmaster. It can carry eight soldiers and is intended as a 'protected mobility' replacement for the VAB; the vehicle is highly manoeuvrable and will primarily be used by units such as the 11th Airborne and 27th Mountain Brigades.

The KMW German Special Operation Vehicle (SOV) is an open-topped light armoured vehicle developed by Krauss-Maffei Wegmann (KMW). The vehicle entered service in 2019 and can be used for long-range reconnaissance and special operations. Sitting high off the ground, the vehicle features an innovative folding roll-bar that reduces the preparation time for airlifting the vehicle in under two minutes. It is air-transportable with weapons stay-mounted for immediate combat readiness operations. The vehicle includes a five-tonne self-recovery electric winch with a 50-foot steel rope.

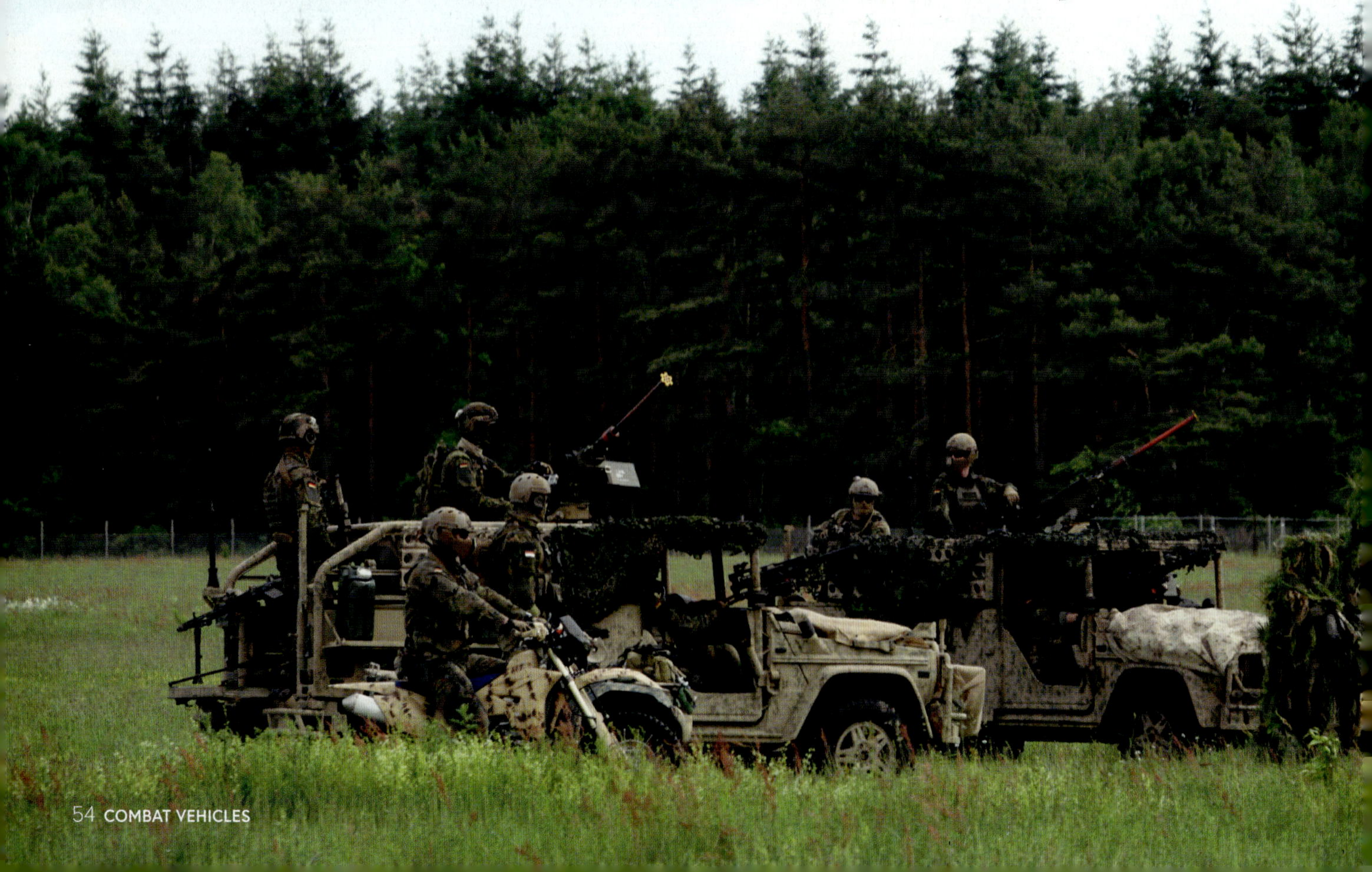

It features three weapon mounts, including auxiliary front and rear mounts that can be fitted with a number of weapons – such as a 12.7mm machine gun or a 40mm automatic grenade launcher on the main ring mount for gunner and two 7.62mm or 5.56mm machine guns on pedestal mounts. The vehicle can be airlifted internally by a CH-47 or CH-53 with weapons in

place, enabling immediate combat readiness after unloading.

The Dutch company Defenture developed the Vector as a replacement for the Mercedes-Benz G280 fleet. The Vector features a rugged central spine chassis suitable for all-terrain operations, along with an independent rear suspension and optional four-wheel independent steering. It is a multi-fuel engine capable of running on diesel or aviation kerosene and has multiple

tie-down points to facilitate vehicle transport by rail, sea, and air, including underslung by helicopter.

Non-standard vehicles

Special operations groups often use NSVs (Non-Standard Vehicles) for a wide range of tasks. These vehicles are usually purchased locally to ensure soldiers can maintain a low profile, blending into the environment, rather than using military vehicles. In the early »

ABOVE: The Australian Bushmaster is seen as one of the most successful armoured strike vehicles.
Australian MoD

ABOVE: In the early stages of the war in Afghanistan, members of the US Army Special Forces acquired some locally sourced 4x4s. US DoD

ABOVE MIDDLE: The British Jackal ('Coyote') platform is currently deployed in eastern Europe. Bob Morrison/DPL

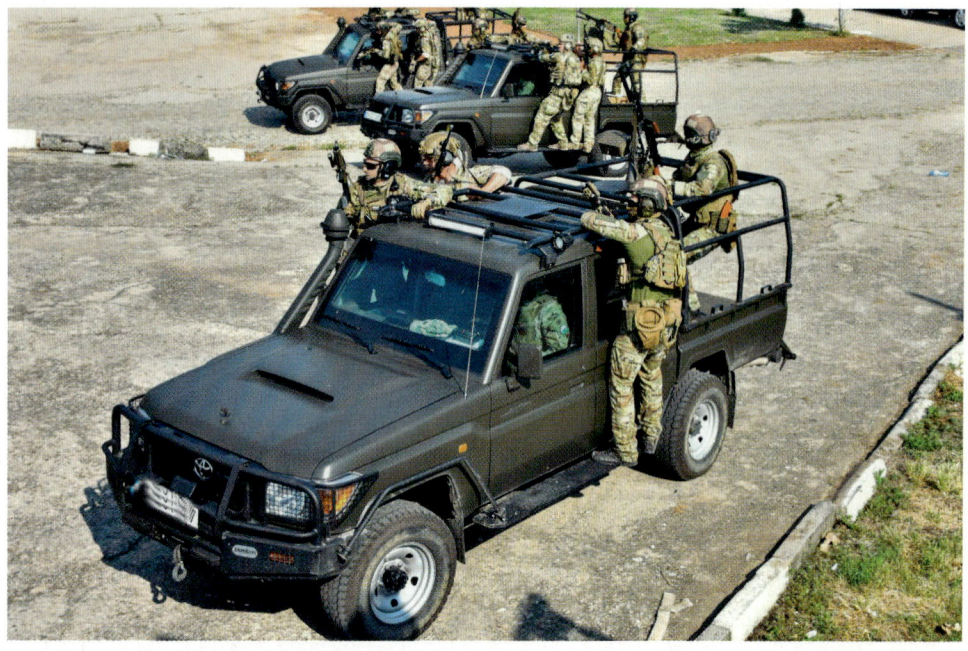

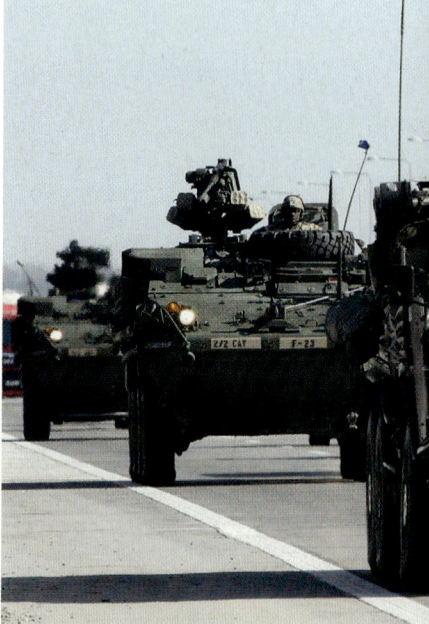

stages of the war in Afghanistan, members of the US Army Special Forces acquired some locally-sourced 4x4s. These were typically Toyota Hilux flatbed pickup trucks in both single and double cab configurations of the type that was used by both the Northern Alliance and the Taliban. The use of these vehicles meant it was relatively easy to source spare parts. These vehicles were fitted with heavy machine guns mounts and, where possible, a roll-bar behind the cabin. Standard headlights were replaced with infrared lamps to be used in conjunction with night vision, while all interior and exterior lights

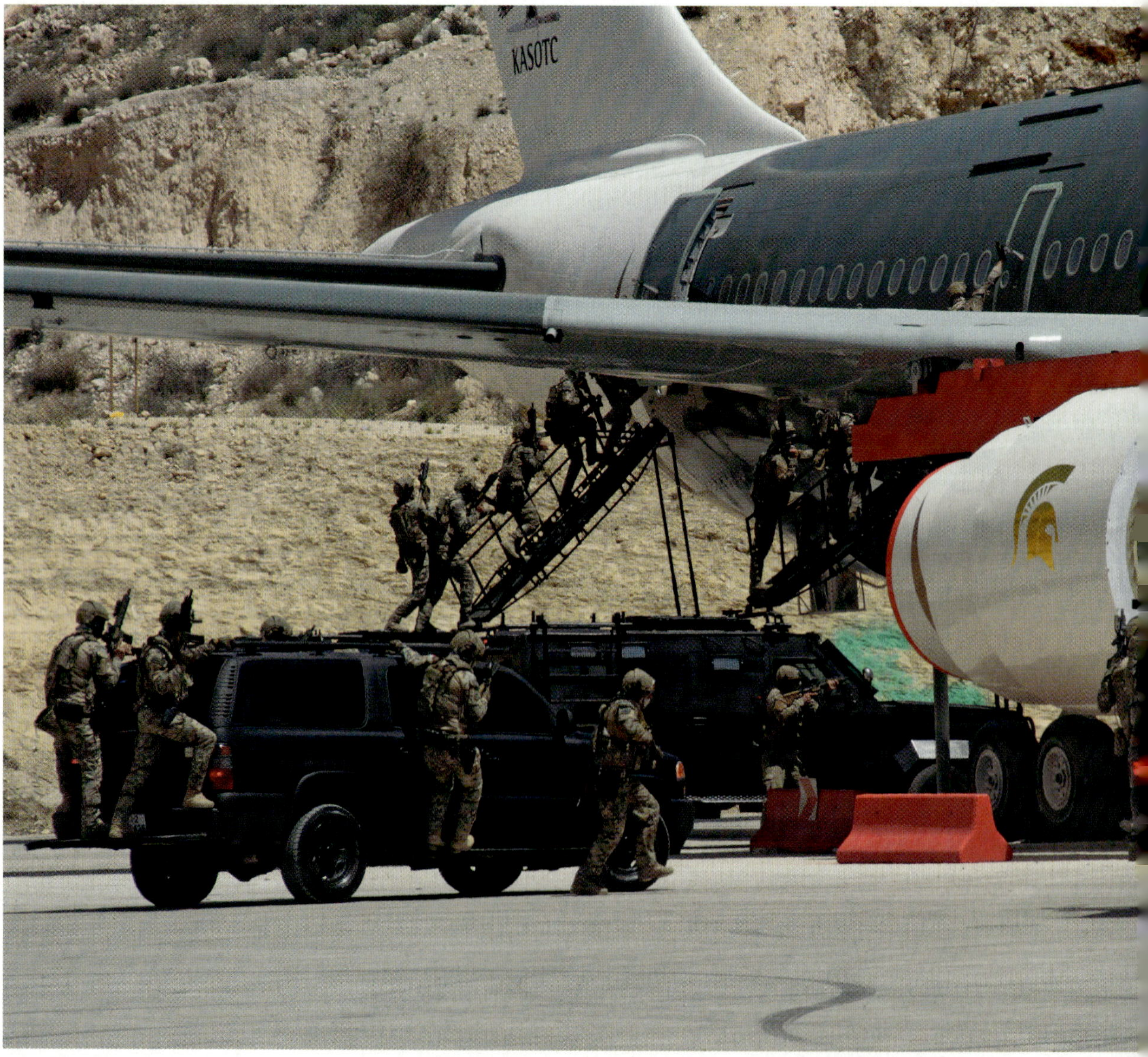

RIGHT: Non-standard vehicles are adapted for hostage rescue and siege breaking by special units. DPL

and brake lights were removed or disconnected as well as any warning seat belt alarms. Army Special Forces also used a number of Toyota Tacomas and Land Rover Defenders in northern and western Iraq during

the initial stages of Operation Iraqi Freedom. These were fitted with mounts for HMGs and grenade launchers. The US special operations' Delta Force mostly used Land Rover Defenders during the invasion phase of the conflict. In areas where sourcing NSVs was a challenge, All-Terrain Vehicles (ATVs) are often flown in on the initial insertion. These small four or six-wheeled vehicles have excellent mobility over rough ground and are equally at home in the Iraqi desert or the mountain paths of Afghanistan. ATVs have no ballistic protection for the riders, but their low profile, speed and manoeuvrability make them ideal for special operations use. It's easier to hide a cache of

ATVs than it is a full-size Humvee or other larger 4x4s. ATVs include a tow hitch to haul a small trailer loaded with ammunition. Engines run on diesel, gasoline or JP8 (standard military fuel). Teams often fitted exhaust mufflers for reduced sound output. Delta Force soldiers are reported to have used electric-powered ATVs that have a very low acoustic signature.

Non-standard vehicles also include a very small fleet of highly specialist and adapted platforms used in hostage rescue from aeroplanes and buildings. Rarely seen in public, these platforms have steps fitted to their sides for soldiers to stand and staircases that can be elevated to access high buildings and aircraft.

ABOVE: Non-standard vehicles can easily be adapted for special operations. DPL

BELOW: Special adaptations to non-standard vehicles allow troops to access high buildings or aircraft at speed. DPL

www.keymilitary.com

£5.90

March 2025

KEY
Publishing

ISSUE 286

CLASSIC MILITARY VEHICLE

UNMATCHED UTILITY

Model Build
1/35 scale
LRDG F30
Truck

*Rare 1944 Buick
M39 Armoured
Utility Vehicle*

Rebuilding a Renault
'Filmstar' R2087 workhorse restored

BRIXMIS on Tour
Cold War spy cars behind the Iron Curtain

300/25

Chapter Six

PROTECTED
COMBAT VEHICLES

Protected 'armoured' vehicles evolved in the post-war years as 'ad-hoc' enhancements to counter both urban and battlefield threats. Sheets of metal were welded to light vehicles in some operations, but the increase in weight reduced the speed of the platform and placed an extra burden on the gearbox. In counterinsurgency operations in Malaya and Aden, innovative armoured measures were added to vehicles in the absence of any factory included armour. Developments in technology to counter asymmetric attacks have seen the introduction of bespoke platforms across both wheeled and tracked vehicles. Wheeled platforms offer speed and have an advantage in urban areas, while tracked vehicles can turn on one track and travel across undulated terrain without fear of being stuck in soft sand, for example. Conflicts in Iraq, Afghanistan, Ukraine, and the Middle East have highlighted the clear advantage of protected combat vehicles in countering Improvised Explosive Devices (IEDs). In modern warfare military forces must be able to shoot and

communicate on the move, preferably from a protected environment and deploy in a range of scenarios, from high-intensity warfare to post-conflict peace support missions, as well as so-called contingency deployments. In the main, both wheeled and tracked vehicles can deliver and evacuate troops to and from the forward edge of the battlefield. They can also mount reconnaissance and surveillance missions to gather intelligence for commanders, as well as providing battle groups with fire support from their mounted weapons.

Warfare Design

To protect occupants from rocket, small arms and blast attacks, protected platforms often incorporate a V-shaped hull to help disperse

LEFT: The British made 'ad-hoc' enhancements to counter threats in Northern Ireland during the co-called Troubles. DPL

RIGHT: The Humber protected vehicle was one of the early troop carriers which was fitted with additional armour for its role in Northern Ireland. DPL

BELOW: The British Snatch Land Rover was ill-suited to the kinetic environment of southern Iraq and Afghanistan. DPL

LEFT: Bespoke factory-made integrated armoured-protected platforms, complete with metal frames to stop rocket propelled grenades, started to be used in service in 2007.
UK MoD

BOTTOM: In the 1970s the South African defence industry had been the first to develop the V-shaped hull and raised the axle height to deflect mine explosions. It took almost 20 years for other nations to adopt the same process.
DPL

the blast and shock of roadside bombs and mines and thus increase crew survivability. Many designs incorporated sloped or angled armour to increase the amount of material a ballistic projectile must pass through in order to penetrate the vehicle and again reduce the lethality of enemy attacks. The V-shaped hull design originated in the 1970s in South Africa and was a game changer. Vehicles such as the South African-built Casspir and the Leopard security platform, both used in the Rhodesian Bush War, were ahead of their time. These four-wheel drive vehicles could carry as many as 12 troops and sat high above the ground »

by commanders. US forces were deployed in Vietnam and in Europe; the 'stand-off' of the Cold War was still focussed on the threat of Soviet tanks swarming into Germany.

Western operations in Grenada, Panama, Northern Ireland, Bosnia, and Kosovo were not seen as presenting a 'high threat' from IEDs that warranted the investment in expensive V-shaped hull vehicles even though counterinsurgencies in areas such as Ulster saw armour vehicles blown up in the border regions.

In 2003 the roadside bomb threat in Iraq and later in Afghanistan forced an immediate increase in armoured upgrades. The Humvee is the most obvious example which received increased levels of protection so heavy that its mobility was impaired. On the streets of Basra in southern Iraq the British Snatch Land Rover was ill-suited to the kinetic environment. Deployment of the vehicle in 2003 was heavily criticised after it came under regular attack. Despite its poor record in southern Iraq, the Snatch was also used in Afghanistan. Then, after the deaths of four soldiers in 2008, including the first female to be killed

ABOVE: The South African industry has continued to innovate protected vehicles which are a favourite with forces across Africa. DPL

to ensure any blast was deflected and less likely to damage the crew compartment. While innovative European nations looked on with interest, they did not invest at the time. In the 1970s UK forces had just embarked on an internal security operation in Northern Ireland and the high wheelbase and V-shaped hull were costly and not seen as a priority

RIGHT: The rise in IED attacks by militia groups in Iraq and Afghanistan forced politicians to invest in bespoke vehicles. DPL

RIGHT: Bolt on armoured packages to vehicles such as the Humvees were defeated with bigger roadside bombs. US DoD

RIGHT: The RG family of vehicles has a proven pedigree of safety with the high wheelbase being a major factor in survivability. US DoD

BELOW RIGHT: The Warthog was procured by the UK government from Singapore Industries and proved highly reliable. DPL

the heavy armoured panels were fitted, it faced power challenges. The BV armoured amphibious tracked vehicle was deployed with the British in 2007, but its limited protection also made it vulnerable, and it was quickly replaced with an Urgent Operational Requirement (UOR) for the Bronco, designed and developed by ST Industries in Singapore. The BV or Viking had no V-shaped hull and carried limited armour, while the Bronco, later named the Warthog, was promoted as being heavily protected. It consisted of two fully armoured units, front and rear connected by a hydraulic articulated joint. The all-welded steel armoured hull provided the occupants with protection from 7.62mm small arms fire and shell splinters. Critically, the Warthog had a V-shaped hull, albeit low to the ground, and throughout its use in Afghanistan, the UK's fleet of 115 Warthogs survived around 30 direct attacks by IED strikes with no crew fatalities. It was claimed that the relatively low rate of roadside bombs strikes was in part attributable to the design's ability to traverse terrain inaccessible to other wheeled or tracked vehicles. In December 2010, a British Army soldier, L Cpl William Reeks, survived after the Warthog he was travelling in set off what was believed to have been an 110lb IED.

Common Standard – STANAG 4569

In the post war years, the creation of NATO promoted cross-training and inter-operability between »

on operations, Cpl Sarah Bryant, the vehicle was withdrawn from active operations, amid calls for greater armoured protection.

The Pinzgugarer, a four-wheel combat patrol vehicle used by the British, was also subject to attack. It underwent an upgrade but after

ABOVE: The United States purchased the RG-33 from South Africa which remains part of its MRAP fleet. US DoD

RIGHT: The remains of an RG-31 which survived a roadside bomb attack. USMC

RIGHT: The US military fitted the armour survivability kit to up-armoured Humvees. This package included 2in thick glass for the front screen and side windows plus a metal and Kevlar composite bulletproof skin. US DoD

forces. An agreement to use 5.56mm ammunition for assault rifles across Alliance forces was agreed and ratified in 1981. This aimed to ensure that in war, nations could use each other's ammunition. STANAG (Standardisation Agreement) became the universal NATO code for common standards across equipment and weapons used by nations of the alliance. This resulted in NATO forces building their protected vehicles to a common standard: STANAG 4569. This agreement among the 30 NATO members ensures the same protection levels and production standards for occupants of both protected and light armoured vehicles. It ensures that on operations, Swedish, American, and British troops can, for example, be transported in a Norwegian combat vehicle with commanders knowing they have the same protection. This is critical if vehicles are to be deployed in areas of high kinetic activity. In Baghdad, for example, when Coalition forces moved between the green zone and the airport – a distance of five miles along a road referred to as 'the gauntlet' – they knew that all force vehicles from Alliance nations were at the same approved standard.

To meet this standard, mandatory testing and assessment is undertaken to test vehicles against ballistic threats. The vehicle is measured in terms of occupant protection, with more than 90% of the passenger compartment required to be protected. Secondary splinters or

fragments within the passenger compartment are considered penetrations and are therefore

unacceptable. Depending on the vehicle category and protection requirements, the level of armour

is assigned to one of six levels. In addition to protection against artillery fragments, Stanag 4569 also requires that vehicles can sustain multi-hit attacks, with one example being a series of small arms strikes or a combination of roadside bombs and light calibre ambush. But while this has been tested, the reality is that militants can increase the size of their IED or mount attacks with armour piercing ammunition. For transparent areas of ballistic glass – seen in most Mine Resistant Protected Ambush (MRAP) vehicles, the multiple-hit test for levels is conducted using a pattern of attack to test strength. Vehicles such as the Cougar deliver the highest level of protection, but even these platforms have succumbed to an IED blast – although they have proven reliability in saving life

Protected Development

In the early 2000s, both Coalition commanders identified the urgent requirement for more enhanced protected platforms as daily IED attacks increased. In a similar situation to the British Snatch Land Rover, the US Humvee was, despite its initial upgraded armour, still vulnerable to roadside attacks. The US fitted their armour survivability kit to 'up-armour' Humvees. This package included 2in thick glass for the front screen and side windows plus a metal and Kevlar-composite bulletproof skin. The underside of the vehicle was fitted with blast plates for protection against mines and IEDs. An initial order was placed for 1,200 vehicles and on average it would take around four days to add the armour to a standard Humvee. In response, insurgents planted bigger bombs, forcing a further upgrade called the FRAG 5. Although it offered higher levels of protection, the penalty of increased weight was reduced speed. In total 8,000 vehicles were upgraded – with ever more powerful IEDs being used by insurgents. A further FRAG 6 armour kit replaced the original ½in steel armour with 3/8in panels. The underbody protection was also improved, and

ballistic glass was added to the list of protective features, creating a vehicle weight of around 1,500lb.

This Level 2 armour package was deemed to be the most that the chassis could reasonably take for a vehicle originally designed as a soft-skinned personnel and cargo carrier. Although the FRAG 5 and FRAG 6 protection did offer increased survivability for the crew, issues were soon discovered. The armoured doors and overall weight of the vehicle resulted in the doors being jammed shut

after a blast, trapping those inside. A special D-ring was rapidly supplied to enable the doors to be wrenched off in an emergency with the aid of a second vehicle and a tow cable. The US Marines (USMC) developed their own armour package for the Humvee, the marine armour kit (MAK). »

ABOVE: The underbody protection was also improved, and ballistic glass was added to the list of protective features, creating a vehicle weight of around 1,500lb. US DoD

LEFT: The Turkish Kirpi is an MRAP combining a V-shaped hull and monocoque design to counter roadside blasts. Turkey MoD

BELOW: The Boxer combat vehicle, currently entering service with several NATO countries, is an example of how standardisation ensures the same level of quality and protection across the Alliance. NATO

ABOVE: The Cougar was put through extensive tests to ensure the protected cabin could survive a roadside bomb attack. US DoD

ABOVE MIDDLE: Australia's Bushmaster has been a resounding success against IEDs, having been deployed in Iraq and Afghanistan. Australian MoD

RIGHT: In Afghanistan, the Bushmaster survived numerous roadside attacks. Australian MoD

Originally the hardtop Humvees came with a ring mount fitted as standard allowing the vehicle to be armed with a variety of weapon types. The usual armament was an Mk19 40mm grenade machine gun or .5 Browning HMG, each attached via a pintle with 360° traverse. A tow missile could also be mounted using the same system.

US military scientists and designers had reviewed the US combat experience in other conflicts, such as such Mogadishu, and identified the vulnerability of gunners to small arms fire – resulting in further modifications to the ring mount to add an armoured shield. Side and rear armoured panels were soon included in the gunners' protection package which led to the development of a fully armoured turret. Several designs of the turret were tried before the army eventually settled on the O-GPK (Objective Gunner Protection Kit). This included armoured glass side windows and an optional armoured roof panel. As usual, the USMC went their own way and adopted the marine corps transparent armoured gun shield (MTAG) designed by BAe Systems. A collapsible version of this turret was also developed, allowing the shipping height to be reduced for amphibious operations.

The progressive improvements in the Humvee's protection levels, driven by operational necessity, eventually led to the standardised M1151 Enhanced Armament Carrier. This was built on a totally new heavy-duty chassis with an uprated suspension to handle the extra weight of the armour. Power was provided by a V8, 6.5-litre turbo-charged diesel engine and a four-speed automatic gearbox. The military finally opted for two armour packages available;

RIGHT: The Russians appeared to have copied the US MRAPs and built the Ural Typhoon. Russian MoD

the 'A kit' installed at the factory with a bolt-on 'B kit' to improve protection levels where required. Run-flat tyres were fitted as standard with a central tyre inflation system operated from the cab. There were several variants produced, including a two-door cargo carrier, the M1152 and the pick-up version, M1165. A couple of

ambulance variants were also fielded, capable of carrying either two or four stretcher cases.

The M1151 was intended to replace all earlier versions of the armoured Humvee then in service. However, despite the enhanced armour protection, it still proved vulnerable to the increasingly sophisticated

and powerful IEDs fielded by the insurgents. This led to the search for a specifically designed mine-proofed vehicle which culminated in the adoption of what was to become known as the Mine Resistant Ambush Protected (MRAP) platform.

Mine Resistant Ambush Protected

In the early 2000s, the US and UK military were pressing ahead with development plans for improved protected vehicles – the Mine Resistant Armoured Patrol platforms. The Australians developed the Bushmaster which incorporated many of the MRAP characteristics and saw service in Iraq and Afghanistan. In the US, these vehicles were produced to protect against small arms, land mines and IEDs using a combination of design features and materials to protect both the crew and engine compartment against a wide range of attacks. They sit high off the ground and incorporate a monocoque-type design and the V-shaped hull, which had been developed 30 years earlier in South Africa. Among these new platforms was the Cougar, which was produced in a number of variants and purchased by the UK who renamed the variants the Ridgback and Mastiff. These vehicles were seen as the ultimate in bomb-proof protection and became the priority platform when moving troops.

MRAPs were constructed with special armour, often made from a combination of steel, composite materials, and other ballistic materials. The armoured construction was designed to dissipate and deflect the high energy generated in explosions, reducing damage to the vehicle and occupants. The interior of an MRAP is designed to offset the impact of shockwaves on occupants. Special seats »

ABOVE: In the early 2000s the US and UK military were pressing ahead with development plans for improved protected vehicles, known as the MRAP – Mine Resistant Armoured Patrol platforms. USMC

BELOW: The British named the US-produced Cougar the Mastiff and in Helmand it saved many lives. UK MoD

ABOVE: Ejder Yalçin, a 4x4 vehicle capable of carrying six personnel, alongside the Otokar Arma. Turkey MoD

RIGHT: The tracked Bv 410 and 206 have proved ideal for mortar teams who can shoot and scout. UK MoD

enhance survivability by reducing the risk of injuries sustained during an explosion. Some MRAP models incorporate reinforced windows, adding an extra layer of protection against ballistic threats as they help prevent shattering and penetration by debris in the event of an explosion. The use of energy-absorbing materials in the vehicle's construction further enhances protection.

The concept of advanced protected platforms was quickly adopted by other nations, in NATO as well as Russia and China. Turkey, which is currently investing heavily in its armed forces, had developed its own protected vehicles with the Ejder Yalçin, a 4x4 vehicle capable of carrying six personnel, alongside the Otokar Arma, an eight-wheeled platform fitted to ferry up to ten personnel. The Arma has a similar shape and external design to the Boxer eight-wheeled multi-role vehicle developed by Germany and the Netherlands in conjunction with Rheinmetall and is due to also enter service with the British Army. France is introducing new MRAP-style vehicles as part of its modernisation plans – these include the Griffon VBMR, which is described as fully 'bomb-proof', and is currently being rolled out across its Army.

By 2014 Moscow's military chiefs had commissioned its own series of MRAP vehicles with the Kamaz and Ural platforms offering similar protection to the US-built MRAPs. Further east, China's People's Liberation Army Navy (PLAN) had taken delivery of the Norinco

ABOVE: The Bv 206 and 410 variants have proved highly reliable in using the rear tracked trailer of the BV as a baseplate for mortar teams. UK MoD

RIGHT: Russia's Kamaz offered protected mobility as well as a remote weapon station but has proved vulnerable in Ukraine. DPL

BELOW: Turkish Vurans, pictured in the Very High Readiness Joint Task Force, sit in the training field during NATO Exercise Steadfast. NATO

CS/VP3. It has a V-shaped hull and appears to incorporate much of the designs first seen in early US-made MRAPs. South Africa has maintained its expertise in armour protected vehicles and produced a

family of MRAPs with the RG-31, also known as the Nyala, in service with many nations. This 4x4 wheeled vehicle with a V-shaped hull and high ground clearance, is in service with Canada, Nigeria, Indonesia, and Iraqi

Combat Systems

While the primary design factor has been to deliver protection against kinetic threats, modern platforms are increasingly being developed with protected combat systems that can deliver advanced optronics, digital options such as robotics, drones, and electronic warfare to help fight the battle. Weapon stations such as heavy machine gun, mortar, and rocket solutions – some of which are remote controlled – are now commonplace in modern combat vehicles. High-intensity conflict in eastern Europe and growing geo-political tensions around the world, have raised demand for integrated technology that can support land-based platforms to detect, identify and engage enemy forces. For many years, such sensors and aids were only found in heavy armour, but as part of a move towards enhancing survivability, digital capabilities that raise awareness are paramount in the 21st century. These state-of-the-art innovations include optronics that enable commanders to identify hostile forces in day and night conditions at range and from within their protected vehicle. Cloud-based digital systems are being developed that can collate intelligence via unmanned aerial and ground platforms alongside technology which can disrupt enemy command systems through artificial intelligence (AI). Support Weapons, such as mortars, heavy machine guns and anti-tank weapons are important in ensuring the delivery of fire-support at troop, company, and battalion level.

In modern warfare mortar baseplates and Sustained-Fire (DF) positions can quickly be located by enemy forces. The need today is for mobile 'shoot and scoot' capabilities in which infantry weapons can be installed aboard protected platforms either in fixed or temporary options. The Bv 206 and 410 variants have proved highly reliable in using the rear tracked trailer of the BV as a base plate for mortar teams. A new generation of 68mm Rocket System, developed by Thales, can be fitted to the roof of most MRAPs and fired remotely – although in areas such as Ukraine, where anti-drone 'cages' are often fitted to the top of combat vehicles, the use of top-mounted rockets and other systems could be restricted.

Chapter Seven

TECHNICALS AND TOYOTAS AT WAR

RIGHT: During the 2021 evacuation in Kabul, Coalition forces used Toyotas that had been given to the Afghan forces. UK MoD

RIGHT: US Special Operations units regularly use 'pick-ups' as they allow soldiers to 'not look like soldiers' and instead appear like local militia forces. US DoD

BELOW: Insurgents in Mali and Niger use Toyotas and other pick-ups in the open desert of the Sahel. US DoD

The global combat vehicle most commonly seen on the battlefield is the Toyota Hilux. This commercial workhorse is the vehicle of choice for militia groups and terrorists across the globe, as well as being a favourite with Western special operations groups. The Toyota pick-up first came to combat prominence when it was adopted by Somali terrorists in the 1990s. Its robust reliability was later highlighted by the BBC's *Top Gear* programme. Presenter Jeremy Clarkson and his team set out to destroy a Hilux, driving it into a tree, down a flight of steps, dumping it in the sea, hitting it with a wrecking ball and setting fire to it, only to discover that it could still be driven.

The potential of these 'off the shelf' 4x4 vehicles was demonstrated in Mogadishu when US forces attempted to detain the notorious warlord General Mohamed Farrah Aidid. It was here that insurgents mounted heavy machine guns in the rear of their vehicles and used them in firefights against US Rangers in what became known as the Battle of Mogadishu. Aidid's forces had banned international Non-Government Organisations (NGOs) from using their own security as they delivered aid and forced charity organisations to

pay local gunmen in what were listed as technical assistance grants. The term 'technical' was quickly adopted in reference to any vehicle carrying armed escorts – the majority of which were the Toyota Hilux. The 'technical' quickly became the visual indication of a warlord's power across Mogadishu and could be measured by how many vehicles he owned.

The Toyota War

The adoption of Toyotas, or any other pick-up for use as a combat platform, is known as a 'technical'. This term refers to any vehicle which has a mounted gun or missile system in the rear. In Afghanistan, the nickname 'Terry Taliban wagon' was used to describe the insurgents' platforms, but internationally 'technical' is the most common term used. While historians claim the 'technical' first appeared in Somalia during the 1990s, the use by the Sahrawi People's Liberation Army who fought for the liberation of Mauritania in 1960 should not be ignored. Guns were mounted on Land Rovers and used in long-range raids. By 1987 the Toyota was the vehicle of choice for Chadian forces in the conflict between Chad and Libya which was dubbed the 'The Great Toyota War'.

During the so-called 'Troubles' in Northern Ireland, the Provisional IRA used vans and trucks to launch mortar attacks and heavy machine gun ambushes. Today, the technical is the combat vehicle used by militia groups from Yemen to Sudan and Syria. The adoption of small jeep-style vehicles can be traced back to World War Two and the exploits of Britain's Long-Range patrol, as well as the SAS. The military capability of the pick-up was first highlighted during the conflict between Chad and Libya. It erupted in the late

1980s over a border dispute. In the years after World War Two, a Franco-Libyan treaty was signed in 1955 which confirmed French ownership of a mountainous border area known as the Aouzou Strip. Chad later gained independence from France in 1960, and the region became an international frontier between two independent states. Then in 1969 Muammar Gaddafi seized power in Libya and immediately claimed sovereignty of the Aouzou Strip amid reports that the area could be rich in Uranium. By 1985 fighting and regular skirmishes were taking place in the open desert, either side of the mountains. Libya had been aligned with Chadian rebel leaders, who opposed the government in Chad and provided Libya with

critical information about northern Chad's mountainous terrain. But in 1987, Chadian rebel leaders abandoned Gaddafi after a dispute about resources.

As Libya's ally had switched sides, France decided to act and supplied Chad with hundreds of Toyota pick-up trucks. The decision to supply Toyotas and not tanks or armoured vehicles was simple: the pick-ups were less complicated to operate, more reliable, highly manoeuvrable, and cheaper. France provided 400 Toyotas complete with anti-tank weapons, which could be mounted in the vehicles. The Paris administration also gave the Chadian military critical air support, effectively grounding Libya's aircraft, but it was the »

ABOVE: Government forces in Mali with a 50-calibre heavy machine gun mounted in the rear of a pick-up. UN

BELOW: Pick-ups have no protection against enemy fire – these vehicles and their crew fell victim to an assault in Syria. US DoD

ABOVE: The Iraqi police received hundreds of pick-ups as part of an international aid project. US AID

RIGHT: A graveyard of Land Rovers used by the Sahrawi People's Liberation Army who fought for the liberation of Mauritania. DPL

BELOW: A US heavily MRAP crew on patrol with local government forces in Niger, West Africa. US DoD

that had been occupied by Libyan forces in 1986 due to its natural resources such as uranium, which was of interest to Gaddafi and his nuclear armament project. At the beginning of 1987, the last year of the war, the Libyan expeditionary force comprised 8,000 soldiers, 300 T-55 battle tanks, multiple rocket launchers, and regular artillery, as well as Mi-24 helicopters and 60 combat aircraft. However, the Libyan soldiers were demotivated and disorganised. The Chadians, on the other hand, had 1,000 brave and motivated soldiers with neither air support nor armoured tanks of their own – but plenty of Toyotas. Chad could count on the French Air Force to keep Libyan aircraft grounded. More importantly their assault force was armed with Milan anti-tank weapons, supplied by the French government and capable of destroying the Libyan tanks. The combat success of Chad Army's reliance on Toyotas was highlighted at the Battle of Fada in January 1987. Hassan Djamous, commander in chief of the Chadian Army, deployed 3,000 men into battle with his concept of operations being a lightning vehicle-borne strike on Fada, the capital of Ennedi Plateau, in the northeast of Chad. The Commander and his soldiers took the Libyan soldiers and members of the Democratic Revolutionary Council by surprise. In a short but brutal engagement, the Chadian force almost annihilated the Libyan armoured brigade that defended Fada. In total 784 Libyans and militiamen died, 92 T-55 tanks and 33 BMP-1 armoured infantry vehicles were destroyed, and 13 T-55s and 18 BMP-1s captured – 81 Libyan soldiers taken prisoner. Chadian losses were minimal: 18 soldiers died, and three Toyotas were destroyed. This was the first major combat victory which employed the tactic of using light trucks armed with heavy machine guns and rockets.

small pick-up trucks that would prove too much for the Libyans. They swept the desert, attacking military bases in 'shoot and scout' raids catching Gaddafi's heavily armed forces off-guard. The Toyotas might not have had 'the punch' of a tank, but they were small and quick, and difficult to defend against. The last phase of the conflict took place in the disputed area of the north of Chad, an area

Ride of Choice

While the AK47 has, over generations, become the iconic weapon of militia forces across the globe, the Toyota Hilux and Land Cruiser established themselves as the 'ride of choice' for insurgent forces. The widely used expression "there is nothing more expensive than a cheap car" is not true when it comes to the Toyota Hilux. During the 1990s these pick-ups and other similar platforms were widely used across Africa, from Sudan to Ethiopia, Rwanda, and Congo. In addition, they were adopted by Pakistani militants and appeared in conflicts in Nicaragua and El Salvador. In 2000 UK forces were sent in to mount an evacuation in Sierra Leone, which quickly evolved into a peace support mission. The capital Freetown had been under threat from the Revolutionary United Front (RUF) and a group called the West Side Boys (WSB). Both had

little military organisation, appeared to be using old weapons, and lacked basic resources, but they operated a fleet of pick-ups armed with heavy machine guns which gave them the ability to launch surprise attacks on government forces.

More recently the Toyota was widely used by insurgents and extremists in Iraq, Afghanistan, and Syria, where huge numbers have been used to form mobile assault units. The pick-up truck is also in regular use with special operations units – a major factor being that it allows them to reduce their footprint and avoid using armoured vehicles.

The pick-up is widely regarded as the most important force multiplier in modern military history. These vehicles have influenced how insurgencies fight with mobility and mounted weapons. In Afghanistan, the Northern Alliance fitted 80mm rockets pods recovered from a

crashed Soviet Mil Mi-24 *Hind* helicopter gunship into the back of small jeeps – which they then used against Soviet forces, while in the Yemen militants fired missiles to attack shipping and then drive away to avoid being hit by Coalition fighter aircraft.

The mass use of 'technical' vehicles has proved that wars can be won on a budget. More than 300 Toyota trucks can be purchased for the cost of one tank and with four-wheel drive, can operate in almost any terrain. Being lightweight allows them to cross weak bridges and tackle fragile roads that armoured vehicles cannot. The Toyota is also a first choice for many indigenous forces – including Western special forces. At the start of the war in Afghanistan, special operations units purchased scores of Toyotas Tacoma pick-up trucks. They added brush guards, roll bars, machine gun mounts, bumper »

ABOVE: In Afghanistan, the Northern Alliance fitted 80mm rockets pods recovered from a crashed Russian *Hind* helicopter in the back of small jeeps. Yves Debay/DPL

ABOVE LEFT: In the absence of pick-ups, insurgents will often adapt motor cars. Kurdish Military

BELOW: The pick-up is the most common vehicle in Africa used by the military, militia, and international aid charities. UN

winches, and antenna mounts; removed interior lighting, seatbelt alarms and reversing buzzers to make their improvised gun trucks quiet and tactical. The speed and agility of the technical helps overcome the disadvantages of bad intelligence, weak leadership, and the poor planning of dispossessed nations fighting wars. Pick-ups don't require special training to operate. They require no special logistical support, and any country can utilise them. They don't guzzle fuel, and they don't require constant maintenance. If a pick-up breaks down, parts can be sourced. If no parts are available, the view is 'it's just a pick-up truck; park it and walk away'.

While Western armies develop infantry fighting vehicles that can carry a team of soldiers who must be strapped into special bomb proof seats, with no regulation or safety guidelines for technical vehicles, insurgents pack as many fighters as they can into the back of a Hilux. There are numerous reasons why Toyota pick-ups have become the primary vehicles of Third World militias. Countries with poor economies are often saturated with light pick-up trucks which have

been donated by non-governmental organisations (NGOs) such as US AID and procured by militants when the NGOs leave. As part of their training and development of the New Iraqi Army (NIA), the United States supplied hundreds of pick-ups to the NIA in readiness for their offensive to remove Islamic States from Mosul in the north of the country. Many ended up in the hands of Islamic State and Syrian militant groups. There's no doubt these vehicles have transformed the way wars are fought.

Islamic State

The remote areas of the Middle East are ideally suited for the pick-up

because they can carry extra fuel and tyres to sustain their operation. In the early days of the wars in Iraq and Afghanistan, insurgents were seen driving filthy old pick-ups that had undergone years of constant repairs. Then with funding from their illegal networks, insurgents acquired new vehicles from global networks and Islamic State exploited the use of the pick-up vehicle. They evolved from the remnants of Al-Qaeda that had fled Afghanistan after the US-led invasion and were reformed as Al-Qaeda in Iraq (AQI) by Abu Musab al-Zarqawi in 2004. Then, when Coalition forces invaded, the group faded into obscurity »

ABOVE: The pick-up is widely regarded as the most important force multiplier in modern military history. Rockets and heavy machine guns have been fitted to this one. DPL

ABOVE RIGHT: These fighters have used rope to tie the tripod legs of a 7.62mm machine gun to the roof of a pick-up. UN

RIGHT: Militants in northern Mali used pick-ups in their fight against French special forces. UN

LEFT: The pick-up has been used as a platform to fire surface-to-air missiles in Yemen, Syria, and the Middle East. US DoD

for several years, only to rise again in Iraq in 2008. Over the following years, it took advantage of growing instability in Iraq and Syria and with new funding, carried out attacks using an army of Toyotas. The group changed its name to the Islamic State of Iraq and Syria (ISIS) in 2013. Then ISIS launched an offensive on Mosul and Tikrit in June 2014, advancing in hundreds of picks-ups fitted with .50 calibre mounted heavy machine guns. The aim of their leader Abu Bakr al-Baghdadi was to create an Islamic caliphate stretching from Aleppo in Syria to Diyala in Iraq. The Toyota quickly became the 'brand' of the Islamic State when they moved into Syria. Al-Baghdadi needed large numbers of pick-ups to support his operations. The group declared a caliphate and took over vast swaths of territory in Iraq and Syria which it policed with fighters manning huge numbers of Toyotas. Under Al-Baghdadi's leadership, ISIS has secured revenue streams through oil sales from ISIS-controlled oil fields, ransom payments, together with cash and precious metals looted from banks. He attracted fighters from across the Middle East and needed transport to push his terrorist army across Syria. Toyotas were procured and fitted with weapons. As witnessed in other conflicts, the Hilux provided the ability to deliver, seed and surprise in their attacks. But terrorist organisation ISIL (Islamic State of Iraq and the Levant) introduced a new threat – the 'Vehicle-Borne Improvised Explosive device' – a Toyota packed with

explosives to be driven straight into Coalition forces. Al-Baghdadi opted to 'up amour' some of these Hilux pick-ups into a new fleet of combat vehicles which spearheaded these suicide bomb attacks.

The improvised armour was copied by the Kurds who fabricated armoured panels for their pick-ups. ISIL did not have the high-tech machinery or factory resources to produce the armour they needed – instead, they used blow torches, sheets of steel, and initiative. The finished vehicles looked like they had been in a post-apocalyptic movie and these mobile fortresses could be driven straight at a Syrian Army base or Coalition force and ignited. ISIL spread rapidly due to its ability to quickly

incorporate captured weapons, including armoured vehicles, into its ranks and mount new attacks. While these vehicles were fitted with heavy weaponry, much of the fighting was done by IS fighters with ordinary AK-47s and M-16s, firing over the sides of the armour plating. Al-Baghdadi dismissed the concept of modern warfare, with its long-distance air strikes and use of drones, as being cowardly and placed a premium on individual heroism in battle. But the armoured Toyota, like all armoured platforms, sacrificed speed for protection as they were slow, often hard to manoeuvre and easy targets for Coalition fighter jets – as was al-Baghdadi who was terminated by US Special Forces.

ABOVE LEFT: Somali fighters in Mogadishu – it was here that the term 'technical' was first used to describe an armed pick-up. UN

BELOW: In Sierra Leone, the Revolutionary United Front and a group called the West Side Boys widely used the Toyota Hilux. DPL

Toyota Hilux vehicles which quickly became the 'war wagon' of the insurgency against NATO forces. To add to their fleet, they mobilised hundreds of UAZ 469 jeeps that had been abandoned in 1989 and were still being used.

After the 2001 terror attacks on the United States, the arrival of Coalition forces also saw the arrival of hundreds of pick-ups. These were used by Coalition forces at Kabul airfield, by special forces, and to equip the Afghan National Army (ANA) and Afghan National Police (ANP). The Hilux became a familiar sight in Helmand, often leaving Coalition forces facing the challenge of deciding which was an insurgent and which was a civilian vehicle. When NATO forces ended combat operations in southern Afghanistan in 2014, hundreds of pick-up trucks were passed to Afghan National Security Forces (ANSF). Coalition forces then focussed on security in Kabul and by late 2020 Washington announced the »

LEFT: Iraqi police units used steel sheets fitted to the side to provide limited protection for the gunner in the rear. US DoD

The Taliban

In Afghanistan, the Taliban insurgency had followed the principle of warfare that the mujahedeen had used against the Soviets – use any vehicle that you can adapt to your need to mount raids against the Soviets. In June 1979, Moscow mounted an intervention, which they alleged was designed to reinforce the government in Kabul. As they arrived on Christmas Day in December 1979, the military brought hundreds of UAZ-469 jeeps with them. The war in Afghanistan lasted until 1989, when Moscow ordered a withdrawal of its forces – leaving thousands of armour vehicles, aircraft, and jeeps behind. These jeeps were quickly pressed into service along with a small number of Toyotas, many of which had been brought into the country with Western aid development initiatives in the early 1970s, before the Soviets and then the Taliban took grip of the country. Warlords across Afghanistan used these jeeps to mount attacks against regional neighbours in a battle for power in the wake of the Soviet exodus in 1989. Now with its institutions dismantled, the country was totally lawless and could not protect its citizens. In the 1990s a new Islamic group emerged, comprising religious scholars who had studied at madrassas in Quetta, Pakistan, and dedicated their lives to an extreme form of Islam. Headed by Mullah Omar, a former mujahedeen fighter and religious scholar, it became known as the Taliban. As it moved into Afghanistan, the group needed transport and arrived in

LEFT: A seat has been welded into the rear of this pick-up for the gunner and his Russian PKM machine gun. US DoD

BELOW: A pick-up with what appears to be a Russian heavy machine gun mounted in the rear. US DoD

COMBAT VEHICLES

potential withdrawal of US forces – signalling the exit of Western troops from the country. By now there was an estimated 20,000 pick-ups in use by both the Taliban and Coalition forces. Taliban commanders and their 'Hilux Army' took the announcement by Washington that Western forces were leaving as the signal to start a major offensive. Their swept into power across the south, commandeering ANA and ANP vehicles for a drive towards the capital, capturing more Afghan Army bases and their weapons, as well as more pick-up trucks. The Toyota was now fundamental to the speed of the insurgents' offensive and by August 2021 they were at the walls of Kabul. As American and British forces arrived to mount an airlift evacuation of civilians, they opted not to use aggressive armoured platforms. Instead, they used pick-

ups that had been abandoned around the airport which were put to use ferrying evacuees. As the evacuation ended, Coalition forces left Kabul and abandoned millions of pounds' worth of equipment, including hundreds of Ford Ranger and Toyota Hilux vehicles. As television crews filmed the departure, the Taliban toasted their new fleet. Overnight they had secured the newest and biggest army of pick-ups in the world. But it wasn't just pick-ups that the Taliban gained, despite attempts to 'deny' them thousands of items of equipment by destroying it. The insurgents were left with a huge amount of resources, including hundreds of advanced Mine Resistant Ambush Protected Vehicles (MRAPs), as well as the latest Humvee heavily upgraded vehicles, capable of withstanding a roadside bomb.

Chapter Eight

GLOBAL COMBAT VEHICLES

BELOW: US and Turkish MRAPs: Ankara's Kirpi proved very effective against blast bombs in Syria. US DoD

The conflicts in Afghanistan and Iraq focused the demand for a new generation of combat vehicles to counter the Improvised Explosive Device (IED), which has been further advanced by the dynamic of the war in Ukraine. Here, protected, and light platforms have faced new challenges on the battlefield.

The United States' development of Mine Resistant Ambush Protected (MRAP) vehicles in 2007 delivered change for the military, with an ability to defeat most roadside bombs, but today, a new threat has surfaced in eastern Europe, overshadowing those bombs. The First Person View (FPV) armed drone allows operators to chase combat vehicles across the battlefield from a safe distance and direct their highly accurate munition directly onto the target with pinpoint accuracy. The US remains the brand leader in combat vehicle technology, with »

RIGHT: The US development of Mine Resistant Ambush Protected (MRAP) vehicles in 2007 delivered change for the military, the ability to defeat most roadside bombs. US DoD

China, Russia, India, and the Gulf states adapting Western designs into their concepts. Today, both protected and light platforms must aim to avoid the enemy in a combat zone that is increasingly packed with sensors able to 'track and trace' any movement and compromise their missions before they reach the target. The MRAP has been a 'trademark' platform for the past two decades as defeating the armed drone has become an urgent issue.

Combat capability

Europe is the biggest producer of combat platforms and while some countries in the Middle East, Asia and the Pacific are now building their own variants, the majority of nations procure their requirements from the international market. Commanders seek combat capability that can be deployed in a range of

ABOVE: The United States remains the brand leader in combat vehicle technology as China, Russia, India, and the Gulf states adapt Western designs into their new concepts US DoD

RIGHT: The Cougar, Caiman, Navistar, and Oshkosh platforms saved a significant number of US and Coalition lives in more than eight years of combat in Iraq and Afghanistan. US DoD

RIGHT: The British used the Cougar, renaming it the Mastiff. UK MoD

ABOVE: South African companies were the first to design and engineer the V-shaped hull back in the 1980s and they continue to set the pace with their high wheel base vehicles. DPL

BELOW: The Kalyani M4 is a high-mobility MRAP produced by South Africa in service in India. Indian MoD

scenarios and environments from desert to arctic. These combat vehicles must be able to defeat modern weapons, but not so heavy that they sacrifice speed… and at the same time must be within budget. The United States military has set the standard in MRAP technology: its MRAP programme is a success story, and the concept of V-shaped hulls is now widely adopted. The Cougar, Caiman, Navistar, and Oshkosh platforms saved a significant number of US and Coalition lives during more than eight years of combat in Iraq and Afghanistan. Around 20,000 MRAPs were deployed to US units and an estimated 27,000 to Coalition forces.

South African companies were the first to design and engineer the V-shaped hull back in the 1980s and they continue to set the pace: the Kalyani M4 is a high-mobility MRAP and one of their latest productions. It is designed predominantly as a protection vehicle with a concept that offers high speed and quick manoeuvrability. It maintains a high wheel base, as is the South

African trademark in mine-protected platforms, and it can carry up to eight people. With all the armour, the M4 weighs around 13 tonnes, but it can easily climb a 43° incline and can wade rivers. The Kalyani M4 uses a turbocharged diesel engine, has a top speed of 80mph and a range of 600 miles. During testing, the M4 was able to withstand three 30lb explosive charges under the wheels and simulated IED blast aimed at the side of the vehicle.

The Indian Army has procured the M4 and describes it as the 'ultimate' mine-resistant ambush-protected patrol vehicle. India is using the vehicle to support its operations in Ladakh where the New Delhi forces are locked in a border dispute with China. South Africa has also developed the innovative Mbombe 6 – which meets NATO's Stanag 4560 standard. This futuristic-looking vehicle has been designed with sharp angles to the hull, aimed to deflect incoming missiles. Its unladen weight is 16 tonnes and it can ferry 11 personnel. The six-wheel platform has a maximum speed of 70mph and a 500-mile range. Jordan, Libya, Ecuador, and Ukraine have procured the Mbombe 6.

The Australians operate one of the most successful designs seen in combat vehicles – the Bushmaster. It was designed and developed by what were then state-owned Australian defence industries, to meet a military requirement for a vehicle that could operate in the remote areas of northern Australia on extended »

patrols and is an armoured upgrade to the Long-Range Patrol Vehicle (LRPV). It bears the hallmark of an MRAP, but it entered service in 1998 – before the US MRAP vehicles. It is mine-protected can survive most known landmines as well as small arms attacks, including armour-piercing rounds. Its V-shaped monocoque hull deflects the blast away from the vehicle and its occupants. It can carry up to nine soldiers and equipment, as well as additional fuel and supplies for five days. Powered by a 7.2-litre six-cylinder diesel-turbocharged engine, the Bushmaster is able to reach speed of 70mph. The fuel and hydraulic tanks of the vehicle are located outside the crew compartment, and it has an automatic fire suppression system. Between 2009 and 2012, the protected mobility troop carrier and the command and mortar variants in

As well as conflicts in East Timor and Iraq, the Bushmaster has been deployed to Mali, Afghanistan, and Syria.
Australian MoD

LEFT: The Australians operate one of the most successful designs seen in combat vehicles – the Bushmaster.
Australian MoD

RIGHT: The Finnish are in the process of replacing the South African RG-32M that has been in service with the nation for many years.
Finland DoD

BELOW RIGHT: South Africa has also developed the innovative Mbombe 6 – which meets NATO's Stanag 4560 standard.
Paramount SA

use in Afghanistan were upgraded. This included the addition of the remotely controlled weapons station, automated fire suppression system and ECM systems. Bushmasters used by Special Operations Task Group vehicles were fitted with a weapon ring to mount a 12.7mm heavy machine gun. Bushmaster is air transportable by the C-130 and CV-17. The vehicle has been deployed on operation in East Timor, Afghanistan, Iraq, Mali, and Syria. It is simple, but its highly robust design has made it a popular choice with armies across the globe including Canada, France, Spain, Netherlands, and the UK.

Finland may not immediately be thought of as an innovative defence manufacturer, but Sisu Auto has designed a four-wheeled, modular, mine-resistant ambush-protected platform (MRAP) suitable for operations in the High North and

across Europe. The vehicle was ordered to replace the South African RG-32M and includes variants for troop transport, air defence, command and control and medical care.

Through the framework agreement between Finland and Sweden for defence co-operation, more than 260 vehicles are planned to be produced.

Combat clones

Costly investment in research and development has encouraged some countries to 'adopt' similar designs that are in service. The Chinese-made Dongfeng EQ2050, for example, is an armoured combat vehicle that looks very much like the US Humvee. Allegedly, it was developed after Chinese commanders saw the US vehicle when it was deployed in the 1991 Gulf War and opted to build something similar. The Dongfeng has been »

upgraded more than six times, with the Dongfeng CSK131 one of the latest variants. The chassis has been completely redesigned with new engine and electronics including on-board computers and digital map software as well as a BeiDou satellite communication and positioning system. But it still looks like a Humvee. It is one of the two principal light armoured vehicles currently fielded by the People's Liberation Army Navy (PLAN). All CSK-131s are equipped with a manually controlled turret.

According to intelligence sources, China is in the process of building a small armoured amphibious platform that would presumably be used in any seaborne assault against Taiwan – the former island that China aims to reunify with the mainland. Taiwan lies roughly 100 miles off the coast of southeastern China; Beijing also wants to reinstate its jurisdiction over the 22 islands in the Taiwan group and 64 islands to the west in the archipelago.

Moscow appears to like the design of the Humvee, too. Its Tigr platform is for many observers a Humvee lookalike and was introduced into service in 2006. Officially designated as the GAZ-2975, it is deployed by rapid-reaction teams and special forces to conduct escort missions, patrols, and counter-terrorist operations. The GAZ Tigr incorporates a conventional layout with an engine forward, a crew »

ABOVE: The modular design of the Tigr allows the conversion of base vehicles into passenger, armoured and cargo platforms.
Russian MoD

LEFT: It was allegedly developed after Chinese commanders saw the vehicle when it was deployed in the 1991 Gulf War and opted to build something similar.
PLAN

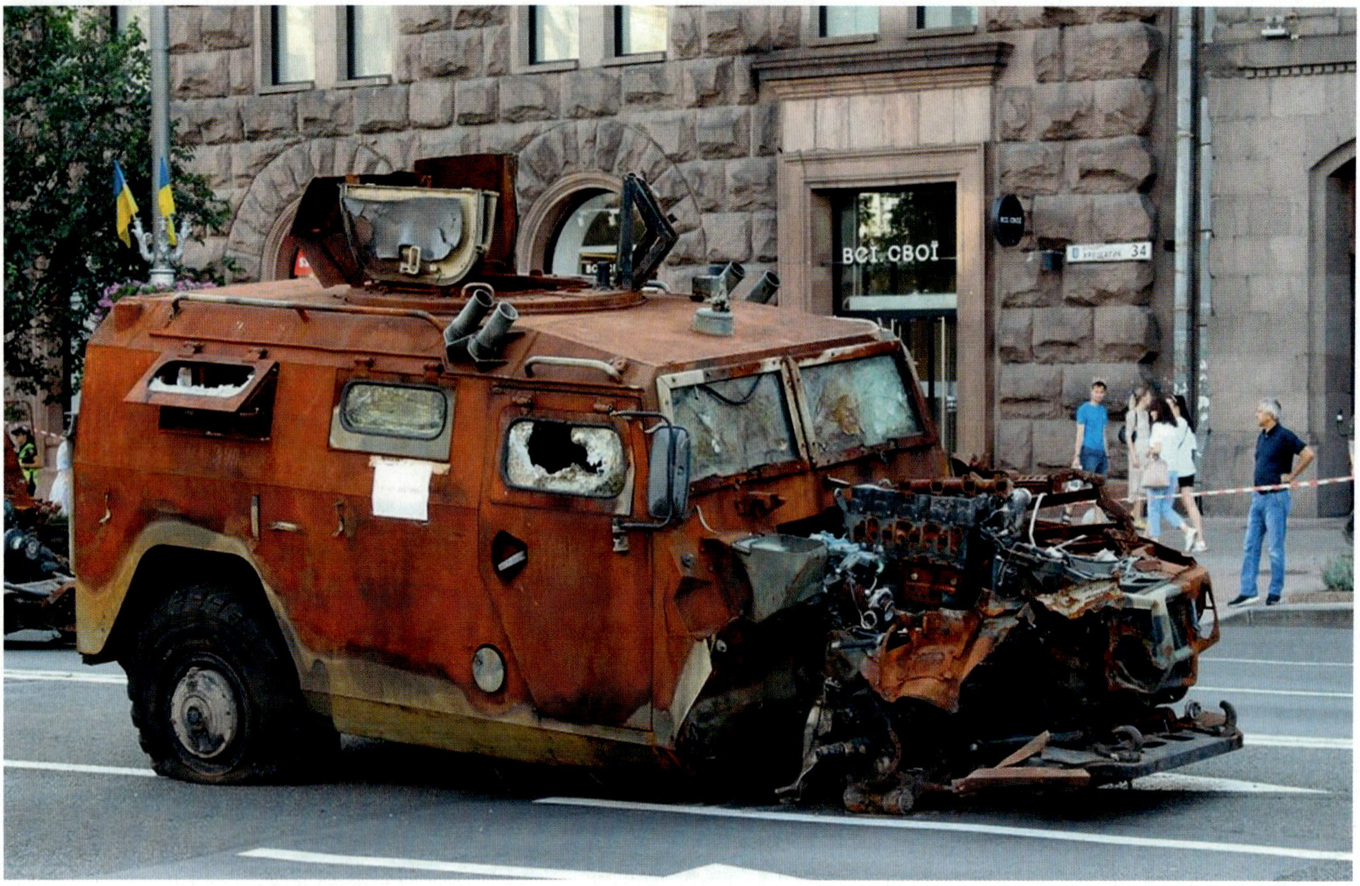

ABOVE: The vehicle strongly resembles the US-made HMMWV. Ukrainian Govt

BELOW: Turkey's Kirpi ('Hedgehog') design incorporates a V-shaped hull and most of the MRAP characteristics. Turkey MoD

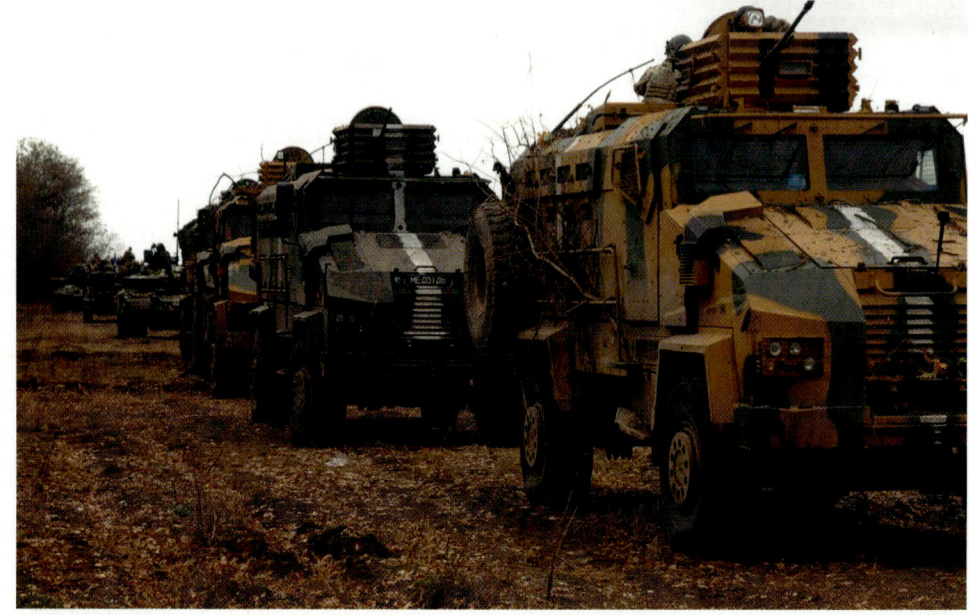

cab in the middle and a troop section at the rear. The modular design of the Tigr allows the conversion of base vehicles into passenger, armoured and cargo platforms. The vehicle can be configured to meet customers' various mission requirements. The vehicle is 16ft long, which increases if adding the vehicle's armour set for further ballistic protection. The standard version of the Tigr vehicle accommodates a driver and 11 passengers. Other variants are equipped with seating for four to nine occupants. The first Tigr prototype vehicles were unveiled in 2002, and production began in 2004. The vehicles are manufactured at the Arzamas Machine-Building Enterprise, part of VPK, in Russia's Nizhny Novgorod region. In October 2012, the Russian Ministry of the Interior (MVD) signed an agreement with Nicaragua to supply an unspecified number of Tigr vehicles. The vehicle was deployed by Russian soldiers during the Crimean conflict between Russia and Ukraine in 2014.

The Tigr-M multi-purpose vehicle equipped with the Arbalet-DM remote-controlled weapon station (RCWS) was unveiled in 2016 and became operational within the Russian armed forces in 2017; it serves to evacuate populated areas while enabling the operator to oversee the situation without risk. The vehicles have been used by Russian armed forces during the conflict in Ukraine to transport infantry and carry cargo. A version of the Tigr-M vehicle was equipped with an open turntable placed on the top of the hull. The Russian Ministry of Defence (MoD) has purchased several Tigr-M vehicles with Arbalet RCWS for airborne troops since 2017; they are designed to enhance the combat effectiveness and agility of reconnaissance teams and are also used by the troops for tactical and fire training. In August 2023, the Russian MoD ordered a batch of GAZ Tigr-M vehicles with additional armour, and these can accommodate two crew and seven landing troops. The vehicles will provide support in patrolling, firing, infantry transportation, reconnaissance, and escorting convoys.

Innovative concepts

Turkey wins the prize for its modern, state-of-the-art design in combat vehicles. The country's manufacturer BMC has developed a series of military vehicles that have seen service in Syria. The Kirpi ('Hedgehog') incorporates the standard V-shaped hull and most of the MRAP characteristics.

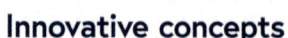

ABOVE: Turkey wins the prize for modern, state-of-the-art design in combat vehicles. *Turkey MoD*

BELOW: Turkey's Elder Yalçin features camera sensors for the crew and a remote weapon station. *Turkey MoD*

Turkish land forces have used the Kirpi 1 intensively on its operations and quickly noticed a reduction in casualties. Sales rose to top 1,500, with more than 200 for export customers. The BMC Kirpi has a front-mounted, hydraulically operated, self-recovery winch and meets the NATO Stanag 4569 standard, but protection levels are classified.

In a second generation of the vehicle, the Kirpi 2 has composite add-on armour and further increased mine-protection. The cabin can carry 13 personnel; driver, commander and gunner facing front, with the ten passengers facing each other along the side walls. Each person has mine-protected seating, gun racks and gun ports to counterfire, if needed. There are two roof hatches, one on front opens up inside the covered manual turret, which can be replaced with an automatic weapon station.

The second roof hatch is at the far end of the cabin. There is a hydraulic operated door at the back of the vehicle, and ten personnel can mount up or evacuate from this door.

BMC also produced the Vuran, which is also an MRAP vehicle. From a distance it looks similar to a Bushmaster, but it sits higher off the ground and is longer. The Vuran features two side doors and a rear cabin access and includes remote »

interceptor, to respond to any incursion by Beijing's forces along its coastline. The unarmoured, four-wheel-drive Special Combat and Assault Vehicle (SC-09A) was manufactured in Taipei, with an initial contract for 56 vehicles for the 871 Airborne Group under part of the country's Special Forces Command. The three-seat vehicle is fitted with puncture-proof wheels, an anti-blast fuel tank, night vision equipment and a searchlight. The vehicle has passenger and rear gun mounts that can be fitted with MK-19 40mm grenade launchers and T-74 machine guns. The SC-09A can be carried on C-130 Hercules transport aircraft and CH-47SD Chinook transport helicopters. Taipei also operates the US Humvee

ABOVE: While the Saxon was initially seen as a major enhancement to infantry protection, the high centre of gravity quickly caused stability problems. DPL

BELOW: Taiwan's unarmoured, four-wheel-drive Special Combat and Assault Vehicle (SC-09A) was manufactured in Taipei. Taiwan Army

cameras to provide battlefield vision for the commander, the only area of concern being the spare wheel that is mounted to the rear with no protection against lethal fire. The Ejder Yalçın, 'Dragon', is a family of armoured vehicles produced by Ankara's Nurol Makina defence manufacturer and includes two versions under the Ejder name: a 6x6 version and the more popular 4x4, the Ejder Yalçın. Production of the vehicle began in May 2014. It features a V-shaped hull design, integrating floating floor plates and blast mitigation seating to provide protection against mines

and IEDs. It can accommodate up to 11 personnel and carry a payload of up to four tonnes. The vehicle is equipped with optionally integrated, remote-controlled, and manually-operated weapon stations and has two-gun ports on the roof. The optional armament mounted on the vehicle includes 7.62mm and 12.7mm machine guns, a 25mm anti-aircraft gun and a 40mm automatic grenade launcher.

For the past two decades, Taiwan has been shaping its forces to defend against an invasion by mainland China. It has built a three-man vehicle, ordered as a potential

in the anti-tank TOW (Tube-launched, Optically tracked, Wire-guided) missile carrier role. The BGM-71 is a small weapon that has been upgraded since the TOW first entered service in 1970.

Combat fails

In June 2024, the Bolivian military discovered that Chinese military combat vehicles are now always what they appear, despite the clever marketing. The PRC Tiger 4X4 armoured carrier was one of many deployed by the army during a suspected coup attempt by a small force that was quickly overpowered. The Tiger 4×4, produced by Baoji Special Vehicles manufacturing in Shaanxi Province is designed to transport infantry and operate

BELOW: After Kirpis started to be operated, Turkish Land Force casualties reduced significantly.
Turkey MoD

in hostile areas with the ability to fit enhanced armour. The vehicle can be adapted for various roles, including command post, law enforcement, riot control and ambulance and frontline operations. The promotional sales material describes it as robust and able to cope with all terrains, but when one of the Tiger armoured vehicles mounted a kerb the steering tie rod broke, leaving embarrassed soldiers struggling to repair the damaged wheel. Previously, Russian President Vladimir Putin was left red-faced when he visited the production line of a series of locally made upgraded offroad vehicles in 2016. As an officer demonstrated their quality, he accidentally pulled off the door handle, which fell on the floor.

The British manufactured Saxon combat vehicle, officially listed as the AT014, looked futuristic in its design when it was announced in the 1970s. It came into service in the early 80s with the British Army as a means of providing protected mobility for personnel deploying from the UK to the Continent in response to a Warsaw Pact invasion. It was built on the chassis of the Bedford TM series truck – then the main utility vehicle of the British Army. At first sight it appeared high off the ground and well protected with a steel armoured shell. It was deemed cost-effective and, by using an existing in-service vehicle, ensured commonality in spare parts and maintenance, thus reducing life support costs. While the vehicle was initially »

viewed as a major enhancement to infantry protection, the high centre of gravity quickly caused stability problems on exercises in Germany. Modified versions were used in Northern Ireland where riot fences were welded to the sides of the Saxon. In the Balkans, there were more concerns: the vehicle easily rolled over on a narrow, high, mountain road and fell victim to mine strikes. In Afghanistan, it was deployed to Kabul and used to ferry troops from the airport to a nearby base called Camp Souter. The vehicle, basically a steel hull welded onto a standard truck chassis, was given a speed restriction to avoid accidents and could not be fitted with extra armour without an engine upgrade. Inside there was little comfort or added extras to counter an IED blast. When the Saxon was sent

to Ukraine, a senior British Army officer said: "They are quite useless, semi-armoured lorries that should be nowhere near anyone's front line. They were withdrawn from Iraq and never deployed in southern Afghanistan." To be fair, the Saxon was the perfect platform in Northern Ireland when rioters were throwing bricks and bottles, but like the Snatch Land Rover, those who sent it into battle were perhaps sat in a nice warm office and had unrealistic expectations of its ability.

In a second fail, the British Army procured the Iveco LMV as the Future Command and Liaison Vehicle (FCLV). With a combat weight of 7.2 tonnes when armoured to the appropriate Stanag level, the Panther was not and was never intended to be a large vehicle; it was, after all, primarily conceived

as a replacement for the likes of the Ferret Scout Car, the CVR(T) Spartan and armoured Land Rovers that were themselves pretty cramped. Although in theory the Panther could have been configured to seat five soldiers, with their kit being carried in the unarmoured rear cargo area, as a command vehicle it needed to be configured to accept the problematic, heavy, and overly bulky Bowman communications system inside the protected crew compartment – a requirement that had not been thought-out by those who designed it. It is claimed by experts that the 'Bowman radio' was the vehicle's Achilles Heel and left the British Army unable to field the vehicle, the radio system, and the crew – due to lack of space. This may have been the reason why commanders decided

BELOW: The British Army procured the Iveco LMV as a Future Command and Liaison Vehicle.
ISAF

to withdraw it from service and the entire fleet being advertised for sale by the UK Defence Equipment Sales Authority in 2018, despite it only being ten years old. Similarly, most of the Land Rover Defender 90 Wolf fleet was retired long before

it's out of service date (OSD) as, unlike previous communications packages that could easily fit in short wheelbase Land Rovers, the Bowman could not fit in the Wolf 90, as there would be no room for even one operator in the back.

ABOVE: The Panther was used as a command vehicle, but needed to be configured to accept the problematic, heavy, and overly bulky Bowman communications system. ISAF

LEFT: When one of the Tiger armoured vehicles mounted a kerb, the steering tie rod broke, leaving embarrassed soldiers struggling to repair the damaged wheel. US DoD

Chapter Nine

COMBAT VEHICLES IN BATTLE

Western nations have developed a fleet of protected and light platforms which were deployed on operations in Afghanistan and Iraq. More recently, conflict in the Middle East and eastern Europe has seen the value of protected vehicles in high intensity warfare in both Gaza and Ukraine.

Where Moscow expected their vehicles to overwhelm Ukrainian forces in days, instead Putin's forces suffered badly against weapons such as the N-LAW and the Javelin light anti-tank system that Ukrainians used to destroy advancing Russian platforms. Teams from Moscow have recovered heavily armoured Humvees for examination after identifying that even when they crippled them, the vehicle's main passenger cabin remained protected from high velocity rounds and missiles.

Since their attack on Israel in 2023, Hamas has adopted tactics of drawing the Israeli Defence Force (IDF) into areas where they can trap and attack them with roadside bombs or rocket propelled grenades. This forced the IDF to review both its strategy and tactics.

In both Ukraine and Gaza, the drone has changed the tactical approach of commanders when they deploy combat vehicles. »

ABOVE: Russian vehicles expected to overwhelm Ukrainian forces but suffered badly against weapons such as the N-LAW Javelin light anti-tank system. DPL

ABOVE RIGHT: Since the start of the conflict in Gaza, Hamas has adopted tactics of drawing the IDF into areas where they can attack with roadside bombs or rocket propelled grenades. IDF

RIGHT: The value of protected vehicles in high intensity warfare has been evident in both Gaza and Ukraine. DPL

Global conflicts

War in eastern Europe is escalating demand for innovative platforms, both wheeled and tracked, with some nations clearly sending vehicles to Ukraine see how they perform in modern combat. The Geneva Academy of Human Rights reports that there are currently more than 100 conflicts underway across the world. As well as the major wars in Ukraine and Gaza, offensive action has been seen in South Ossetia and Georgia, Armenia and Nagorno Karabakh. In central Europe regional tension between Serbs and Albanians on the Kosovo border continues, with NATO overseeing security. The Kosovo Force (KFOR) is a NATO led initiative directed to maintain peace and stability in the region. It involves troops from the alliance rotating a 3,500-strong capability every six -months. Italy has deployed its Iveco protected vehicle there, while the US uses the Humvee, and the UK operates the Foxhound. Here the risk of IEDs is seen as low, but protection is still needed as public disorder has occurred on several occasions. The Middle East and Africa has more than 40 disputes which range from border and ethnic clashes to full scale high intensity warfare across Israel and Gaza, with the threat of an escalating regional war as Hezbollah, the militant group elected to government in Lebanon, attacked Israel, sparking a response from the IDF as the Houthis in Yemen launched ballistic missiles into Israel. In early 2025, the first signs of a peace process started to emerge as it became clear Iran was no longer prepared or able to continue its supply of weapons to Hamas, Hezbollah, and the Houthis. A three-stage process was unveiled which offered hope for the future.

Some of these global clashes are caused by climate change as nations seek to secure water resources. Egypt has accused Ethiopia of threatening its supply of water from the Nile. Ethiopia has confirmed that it has finished filling the reservoir at its

BELOW: N-LAW anti-tank missiles have been used with great effect against Russian vehicles. UK MoD

ABOVE: The British Foxhound has been deployed to Kosovo as part of the NATO security reinforcement package. UK MoD

ABOVE RIGHT: The US Humvee is used by countries such as Iraq and, more recently, Afghanistan. US DoD

giant new dam, which draws water from the Nile. Other tensions are ignited by corrupt governments, the spread of Islamic extremism, right-wing nationalism, and disputes over the sovereignty of land. Africa currently has armed confrontations in Burkina Faso, Cameroon, the Democratic Republic of Congo, Ethiopia, Mali, Mozambique, Nigeria, Senegal, Somalia, South Sudan, and Sudan. Here several countries have procured combat vehicles from Western powers or regional allies.

The United Arab Emirates (UAE) has, for example, supported the Sudan government with the Spartan armoured combat vehicle, which is manufactured in the UAE and incorporates MRAP capabilities, allowing it to withstand ballistic attacks, grenades, and land mine blasts. The Spartan can be used in a wide variety of applications, including police and security operations. Its welded steel body is mounted on the chassis of a Ford F550, a large pick-up made in the US. A variant of the Spartan has also

been produced by Ukraine under licence, called the KrAZ-Spartan. It is currently being used in the war against Russia. The Ukrainians have also developed an unmanned version of the Spartan, although it is unclear if is has entered service and is being used in the war.

In Somalia, the African Union is mounting a support operation with soldiers from Ghana, the Gold Coast and Kenya delivering peace and stability. They are using the South African Casspir and Puma, both mine-resistant ambush »

RIGHT: The Javelin has been used against some of Moscow's most protected platforms. US DoD

protected (MRAP) vehicles. The Casspir has been in service since the 1980s and its four-wheel drive platform can transport a crew of two plus 12 additional soldiers and associated equipment. It was unique in design when launched, providing what was a state-of-the-art defence against mines. The main armoured steel body of the vehicle is raised high above the ground and this design remains in use today. The main thinking behind the Puma was to develop a low-cost and robust mine-protected vehicle without compromising crew safety and quality. Officially listed as the M26-15, the Puma is a vehicle that can be deployed successfully and safely in the harsh environments of Africa and other developing regions.

Western forces have supported regional governments in west and central Africa after requests to the United Nations (UN) to maintain stability in Mali and Niger. France, Britain, and the US have deployed forces to Mali and Niger in a move to counter Islamic State insurgents. The American forces operated independently from the UN and used pick-ups and Polaris light strike platforms to maintain a low profile, while the British used Jackals in long-range patrols around townships. However, a deteriorating situation in which French armoured combat vehicles were attacked and destroyed forced Western politicians to withdraw their military contingents.

In Asia, the Geneva Academy of Human Rights noted that there are regional conflicts taking place from Afghanistan, where the Taliban have

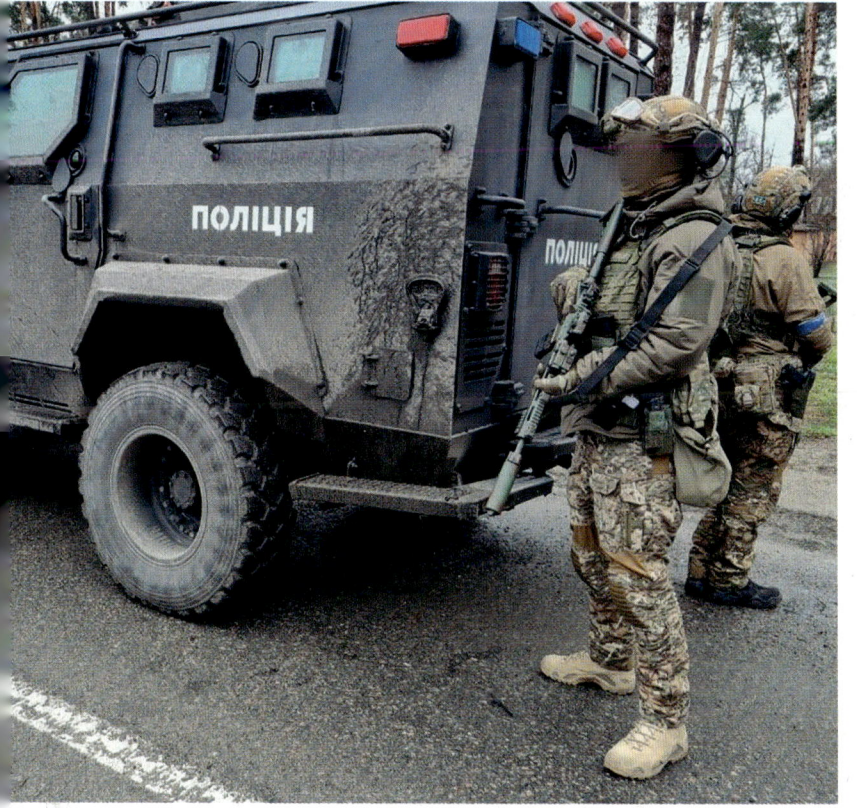

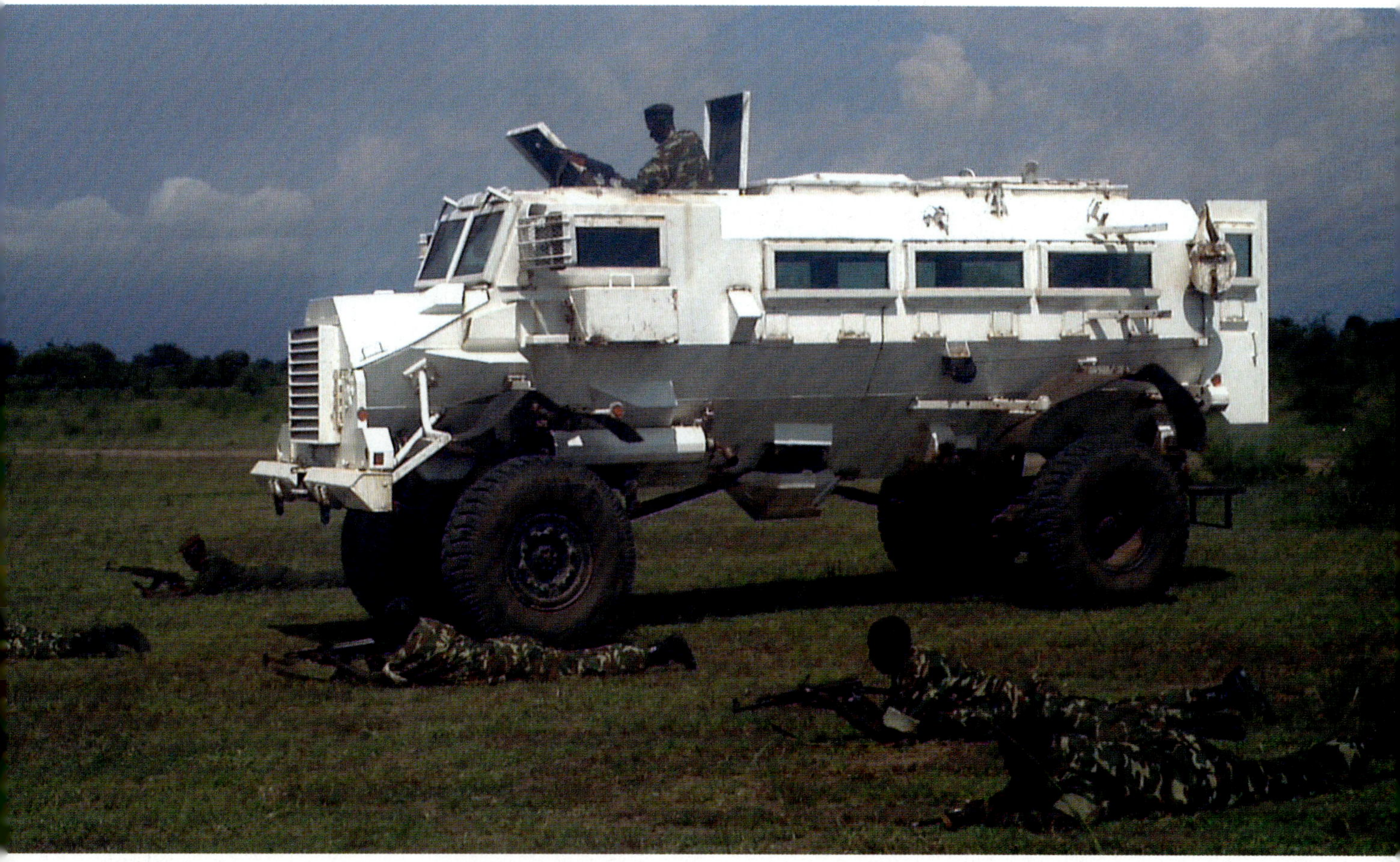

recently attacked Pakistani troops on the border. In addition, there are international disputes between India and China, as well as India and Pakistan. In Latin America, armed conflicts continue to flare in Mexico and Columbia, where cartel gangs fight for power

The Middle East

Hamas used motorbikes and Toyota pick-ups to mount their assault in Israel on October 7, 2023. Since then, the armoured capability of vehicles used by IDF has been tested to the limit. After the initial assault on Gaza by Israeli armoured brigades, the strategy was to move troops forward to hold areas and then police them with a second wave of troops in combat vehicles, with the main aim being to capture any Hamas fighters remaining in the area. However, as commanders switched operations across Gaza to catch Hamas militants off-guard, these fighters moved in behind the departing IDF units, planting IEDs and setting up ambushes which were activated when the IDF moved back into the area. IDF commanders opted to increase the volume of vehicle borne patrols and maintain them in one location, which saw an increase in Hamas attacks These platforms included the MDT David, the Humvee, the Plasan SandCat and the Wolf patrol vehicle.

The MDT David is a light armoured combat vehicle based on the design of the British Land Rover Defender and the Toyota Hilux. Its armour provides protection from small calibre weapons and IEDs, with additional protection built into the roof to counter grenades dropped from high budlings or drone strikes. Built by the MDT Armor Corporation, a US subsidiary of Shlador Limited, the MDT David has been in service since 2007, with more than 400 currently deployed. It has a four-cylinder, turbocharged inter-cooled diesel engine, and can accommodate four to six fully armed soldiers. It has three doors »

ABOVE: The South African Casspr is in wide use across Africa. Henred Fruehauf

LEFT: Kyiv is building the Spartan under licence and deploying it against Russian forces. Ukrainian MoD

and a roof hatch and has survived Hamas numerous attacks, although on several occasions huge bombs have been used to overcome the vehicle's armour. The Humvee is in widespread use by the IDF, with the majority of the variants being fully armoured. At the start of the conflict a small number of standard Humvees were blown up in roadside attacks by Hamas militants of the al-Qassam Brigade in the Netzarim corridor, the area which splits the Gaza Strip down the middle and is located just south of Gaza city, stretching Israeli border to the Mediterranean.

The Plasan SandCat is a composite armoured vehicle that was designed and manufactured in Israel. More than 700 SandCats have been produced since it entered service in 2004. The vehicle has undergone numerous upgrades, and the fourth-generation vehicle is a mine-resistant light patrol vehicle (M-LPV) with a fully structural monocoque frame. The key benefit of this design is a greater level of underbody blast protection without increasing its height, centre of gravity or weight. Israel has also developed the Wolf heavily armoured personnel carrier for urban operations. Produced by Carmor, it is capable of defending against assault rifles, mines and IMDs. The Wolf, like the UAE-designed Spartan, is based on the

ABOVE: French armoured combat vehicles were attacked and destroyed in Mali and Niger. UN

LEFT: The Puma derivative of the Casspir on operations with the African Union. AU

RIGHT: In parts of Africa, European troops on United Nations duty have used pick-up trucks. UN

chassis of the Ford F550 and is powered by a V8 petrol engine. Currently there are 300 in service.

Elsewhere in the Middle East the administration in Saudi Arabia has created one of the most powerful fleets of combat vehicles in the region, procuring the French Sherpa light scout platform, the Georgian manufactured Didhgori Medevac armoured ambulance, the US Oshkosh M-ATV and Humvee, the Spanish URO-Vamtac and the Turkish Cobra II. In November 2009, Royal Saudi, Bahraini ands Qatari forces launched a sweeping ground offensive against Yemen's Shiite Houthi rebels using Turkish Yörük light armoured vehicles. Their low weight and mine and ballistic protection made them superior in operations. Other platforms deployed included the Russian Kornet-D platform fitted with an anti-tank missile system and the US Oshkosh. Meanwhile, the Houthis used small vans to mount rockets to attack ships in the Red Sea, which also provided high mobility against Western air strikes. A major display of Toyota capability was seen in Syria in late 2024, when Abu Hassan al Hamwi's HTS group moved at speed to remove dictator Bashar al Assad. The move to overthrow Assad was secured in days thanks to the mobility of the HTS force, which used hundreds »

of pick-ups and Humvees which had earlier been captured from Iraqi forces. As HTS advanced, Russian combat vehicles were seen exiting the battlefield and driving towards air-bases and ports around Latakia.

Eastern Europe

When Russian invaded in February 2022, the Ukrainian military had a strong but limited force of combat vehicles, mainly focused on legacy Soviet platforms. As fighting erupted, NATO countries quickly supplied equipment to Kyiv. The UK provided Husky tactical support vehicle (the UK version of the US MXT-MV), as well as the larger Wolfhound and Mastiff patrol vehicles which had both proved highly reliable against mines, IEDs and rocket strikes. The Husky is a 4x4 protected highly mobile armoured combat vehicles which entered service with the US in 2006 and the UK in 2010. The roof of the vehicle is fitted with an open-top weapon station that can be armed with a 7.62 mm or a 12.7mm machine gun. The Husky had been ordered by the British Army in 2009, to replace the British Army's Snatch Land Rover in Afghanistan. A total of 262 vehicles were initially ordered and, in 2010, there was a follow-up order for an additional 89. In April 2022, the UK approved the delivery of 120 armoured vehicles to Ukraine, including 100 Huskys.

The US supplied Ukraine with fully armoured Humvees, as well as MaxxPro MRAPs and Styker infantry vehicles. In a social media post, Russian troops can be seen firing high calibre rounds at a disabled Humvee that appeared to have lost a wheel in a mine strike.

ABOVE: The British force deployed in Mali supported the mission using Jackals in long-range patrols around townships. UK MoD

LEFT: The MDT David is a light armoured personnel carrier based on the design of the Land Rover Defender and the Toyota Hilux. IDF

LEFT: The Wolf armoured personnel carrier in use in Gaza. IDF

The soldiers cannot believe how good the protection is on the Humvee and can be heard saying how hard it is to penetrate the glass windows and doors. The Humvee armour has proved 'life saving' in numerous attacks in Ukraine, but large mines have caused injuries to those inside.

Overall, Humvees and MRAPs have been invaluable to the Ukrainian military, with their reputation for protection against a wide range of weapons. As well as for patrols and reconnaissance, some of Ukraine's units are known to have used Humvees in a fast attack role. In addition, an experimental US Army howitzer is being used in combat by Ukraine troops. The 2-CT Hawkeye is a combination of an AM General Humvee and a 105 mm gun equipped with soft recoil technology, which allows the vehicle to withstand the impact of the firing.

The Ukrainian government has also supported the development of indigenous platforms, such as the Novator, a fast interceptor with a V8 diesel engine, fitted with armour to counter small arms and blast impact. It has proved highly successful and is supported by the Vatra, a high wheelbase armoured platform produced for the country's Azov Assault Brigade. It was deployed in the Battle for Mariupol and when Russians forces seized the city, »

ABOVE: Built by MDT Armor Corporation, the David has been in service since 2007. IDF

LEFT: The IDF uses the Humvee with a remote weapons station mounted above the cabin. IDF

BELOW: The Plesan SandCat is another of the armoured vehicles used by Israel. IDF

they sent several back to Moscow for test and evaluation. Putin's forces have also captured an unknown number of Novators, which have been seen in use by the Chechen 141st Motorised Regiment.

Among Russia's combat vehicles deployed in Ukraine is the Gaz-2975 Tigr. Developed with China after Moscow initially refused to grant them a full license, 110 Tigrs were delivered to the People's Liberation Army Navy (PLASN) between 2008-2010 and are in service with Beijing's security police. They were deployed in a security role at the 2008 Beijing Olympics and in the 2009 Xinjiang riots. The Tigr was designed to transport troops and various equipment on- and off-road in mountainous, arctic, and desert environments. It has a chassis frame construction, with a traditional layout of front engine, middle crew compartment and rear cargo area. Standard features include power steering, independent all-wheel suspension with hydraulic shock absorbers and stabiliser bars. While it has a V-shaped hull, it lacks many of the MRAP characteristics, leaving it vulnerable to IEDs and Western anti-tank weapons. Its record in operations in Ukraine has been poor – during the 2022 invasion, the Tigr suffered at the hands of Ukrainian soldiers who were armed with N-LAW anti-tank weapons

RIGHT: Turkish Cobra II in service with Royal Saudi forces. RSAF

RIGHT: The Vamtac, a Spanish produced platform, is also used by the Saudi military. Spanish MoD

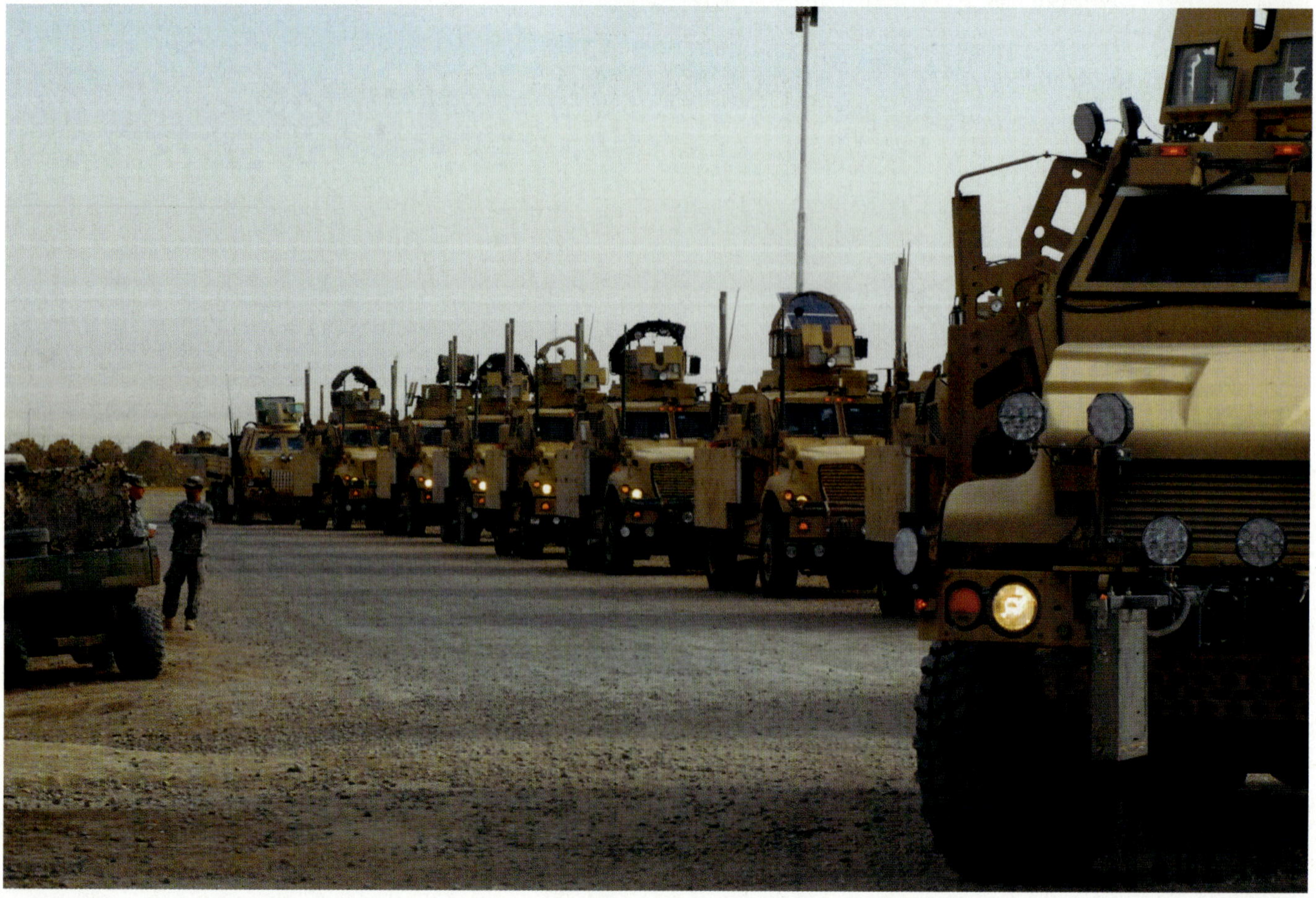

BELOW: US-produced MRAPs are in service across the Middle East, procured by Saudi Arabia and other Gulf states. US DoD

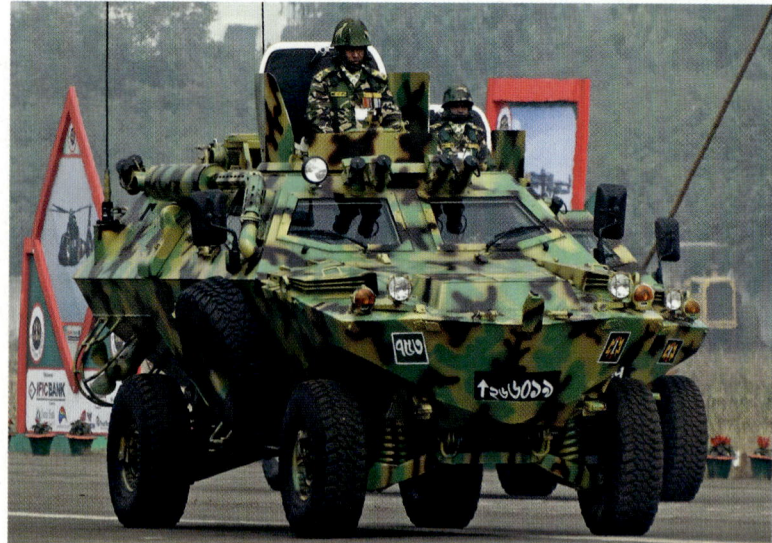

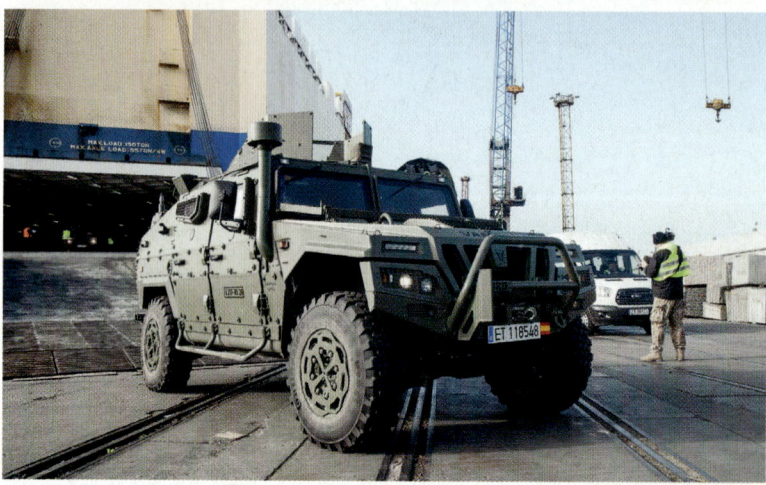

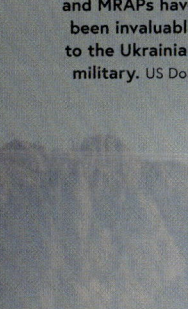

and heavy machine guns who were able to attack and destroy numerous vehicles.

Moscow also deploys the six-wheel turbo-diesel Ural Typhoon in Ukraine. This is Russia's answer to the American MRAP Cougar, a multi-functional, modular MRAP vehicle. The chassis consists of a three-axle drive designed around a high wheeled frame. It is fully armoured and can carry 16 soldiers. Despite being highly regarded by the Russian chain of command, it is another platform that has not performed well in Ukraine, falling victim to drones.

The four-wheel drive Ural Spartak is capable of ferrying eight troops and is considered by Moscow as being able to counter any Western weapon system. The vehicle's frontal armour and roof have been reinforced to withstand 12.7 mm rounds. Additionally, the Spartak can be fitted with additional bolt-on armour to resist 14.5 mm rounds. To counter the threats posed by mines and IEDs, the VPK-Ural has a V-shaped hull typical of MRAP vehicles and is capable of withstanding explosions equivalent to 20lb. In May 2024, a picture of a Spartak was released by the Ukrainian military in which the vehicle appeared to have been destroyed by a drone. At least five Spartaks have also been seen in Iran in what is believed to have been part of a deal in which Tehran supplied drones to Putin's forces.

A third platform deployed by Russia in Ukraine is the Italian-designed Iveco LMV. There is a clear prohibition against supplying arms to Russia due to sanctions imposed following its attacks on Ukraine, but a third party is alleged to have supplied Iveco LMVs to the Russian Defense Ministry. The Iveco uses modular armour packs to adjust its level of protection to its mission requirements, uses suspended seats to keep soldiers safe and has a V-shaped hull to deflect IED blasts. Its exhaust is piped through a cavity in the vehicle's pillars and its turbocharger is located underneath the engine to reduce its thermal signature. Mobility is helped by a run-flat system, allowing the vehicle to move even with completely deflated tyres. Ukrainian attacks have destroyed more than 40 of the 100 Russian Ivecos on operations against Kyiv

A larger fleet of Ivecos was also deployed in Syria, but their current status is unknown.

Afghanistan

Afghanistan lacks a strong government infrastructure, but in 2025 it has one of the largest military capabilities in the region. Hundreds of MRAPs gifted to the Afghan army and police were seized by the Taliban, along with light combat vehicles, helicopters and large stores of infantry weapons and equipment. In total, Taliban forces took control of more than 300,000 light arms, 26,000 heavy weapons and about 61,000 military vehicles, as well as 81 helicopters. Border clashes between the Taliban and Pakistani forces in late 2024 saw the insurgents operating in modern vehicles. Their problem will be in maintaining the resources that Western forces left as parts and spares dry up. The fear is that many will be sold to other militia groups and be used against Western forces.

Chapter Ten

THE FUTURE BATTLEFIELD

Future combat vehicles will be shaped around electric vehicles (EV) and hybrid platforms. This technology will help reduce demand on the logistic supply chain, which is under constant pressure to deliver fuel to the battlefield in order to make sure commanders can sustain their actions. These new fuel systems will also reduce both the thermal and sound signatures of vehicles.

In the United States, GM Defence is working on an EV variant of an infantry patrol vehicle with powerful batteries and solar charging resources to allow it to operate at significant range. Smaller platforms have the potential for innovative plans and could possibly be used for the evacuation of wounded

RIGHT: The UK armed forces formed the Army's Experimental and Trials Group in 2022 with the aim of integrating technology alongside soldiers.
UK MoD

maintenance, but the batteries are very expensive and contain lithium which, in some circumstances, can pose a fire risk due to a phenomenon known as 'thermal runaway'. This is a process in which heat builds up uncontrollably within the battery cells, potentially leading to a chain reaction and causing the battery pack to catch fire or even explode.

Going green

Western forces are running numerous projects to transform the military to electric power, while embracing unmanned ground vehicles (UGVs) as technology shapes the future battlefield. The British Army has commissioned Project Mercury as the overarching plan to incorporate electrification into the future fleet and facilitate further developments in the combat zone. A small number of test-vehicles, the Foxhound and Jackal patrol platforms, have already been fitted with hybrid electric drive (HED) technology. By 2030, commanders expect to see the initial deployment of vehicles, with 2035 being the key date at which most land capabilities will be hybrid or fully electric.

The British Army is currently converting four Land Rover Defenders to electric power before testing them in various battlefield scenarios. Babcock International has been awarded a one-year contract by the Ministry of Defence (MOD) to help the British Army understand the potential constraints of EVs. Partnering with EV experts, Babcock will convert four in-service military Land »

ABOVE: In the US, GM Defence is working on an EV variant of an infantry patrol vehicle. GM Defense

and small-scale resupplies. In Ukraine, electric motorcycles have enabled special forces to carry out reconnaissance without comprising their footprint. NATO nations see green resources as the way forward and, since 2023, the German

military has been developing a hydrogen fuel cell system with the aim being to develop enough power to drive a main battle tank (MBT).

Hybrid engines are seen as a more viable option in the short term. They use less fuel and requires less

RIGHT: UGVs are an evolving aspect of modern warfare. US DoD

Rovers – two protected vehicles and two general service vehicles – from diesel to electric using a drop-in kit and modified battery system. The vehicles will then be put to the test by the Armoured Trials and Development Unit (ATDU) in a series of experimental battlefield and military scenarios, which will assess performance over steep terrain, wading and towing and different climate-related conditions.

With such a large fleet of combustion-engine vehicles currently in service across western forces, the hybrid option is the most cost-effective in the short term. Hydrogen fuel cells are currently seen as being too expensive to produce. The military approach is driven by the need to develop and enhance operational capability ahead of the Russians and Chinese. The change is huge and, as well as the importance of moving away from fossil fuels, scientists are working on other tactical considerations. For example, could an electric fleet of vehicles be brought to standstill by an electronic countermeasure strike and how could these new technologies be used to create an edge over an adversary?

The war in Ukraine has shown how 'green fuel' can be a strategic winner in combat. Commanders assigned to the US Army Futures Command highlighted an incident in 2022 that demonstrates the vulnerability fossil fuels. A 40-mile Russian truck convoy was forced to a standstill in the open countryside to wait for a resupply of fuel. This demonstrated the extent to which fuel-dependent vehicles remain a liability, demanding resupply missions to maintain momentum.

In October 2024, the US Army stated it was ready to start test and evaluations of a future electric light reconnaissance vehicle (eLRV). No decision has yet been made as to whether an all-electric or hybrid model is the way forward, but the eLRV is positioned to be the first tactical platform in the US Army if approved. Work to define what the Army needs is well underway and experiments with existing electrified commercial SUVs at Michigan's Joint Manoeuvre Training Centre and Georgia's Fort Moore are due to take place in 2025. Engineers are seeking to match power with desired range, considering the challenges for an all-electric platform in soft sand and water-logged terrain, which will require a bigger battery.

The hybrid offers dual capability, and a separate project is underway to retro-fit US military vehicles. The US Marines (USMC) have expressed concerns surrounding charging EVs and have a separate challenge in that their platforms need an amphibious capability. Commercially available EVs have demonstrated the ability to drive through water without issue, although in a couple of isolated incidents EVs have caught fire in floodwater due to 'thermal runaway' following battery damage. The USMC is continuing with its development and is focused on hybrid engines. The marines are also carrying out trials on a hybrid system for the light Polaris MRZR used by reconnaissance and special

ABOVE: UGVs that are armed can operate ahead of troops and provide suppressing machine gunfire. UK MoD

ABOVE LEFT: Small, highly mobile and able to move into dangerous areas, UGVs will be a key future combat vehicle. NATO

ABOVE RIGHT: The British Army has launched a project to convert two WMIKs Land Rovers to an all-electric system. Babcock

forces and are planning to trial a hydrogen fuel-cell system.

Having seen the success of using electric bikes in Ukraine, the USMC's 3rd Reconnaissance Battalion is carrying out an evaluation of lightweight battery-electric dirt bikes that could carry marines quickly and relatively quietly across a range of terrains.

Unmanned future

The military is adopting technology to advance operational capability with the introduction of ground based autonomous platforms tasked with reconnaissance, logistical support, evacuation of wounded soldiers and carrying weapons. The market for uncrewed ground vehicles (UGVs) is rapidly evolving, with major implications for future military operations.

At its core, the UGV market is driven by the demand for NATO forces to reduce the reliance on

human soldiers and crewed vehicles. Across Europe and the US military, formations are facing a decline in the number of applicants joining the armed forces, making unmanned platforms an attractive alternative for the future. At the same time the heavy loss of life by coalition nations in both Iraq and Afghanistan changed public opinion and ministers are aware that this can impact on their popularity at election time.

In brutal economic terms, UGVs offer a cost-effective solution to increasingly tight defence budgets, reduce risk to life and augment what is a growing recruitment issue across military forces. The US military has several ongoing »

ABOVE: While tracked platforms are widely used across NATO nations, they will need a permanent source of power.
Netherlands MoD

LEFT: The arctic temperatures of the High North will drain lithium ion batteries. UK MoD

FAR LEFT: The British Army have trialled a system which deploys behind troops, carrying heavy equipment and additional supplies.
UK MoD

ABOVE: At present, vehicles can carry extra fuel strapped to the rear of the vehicle, but in the future, they may have to carry extra batteries.
Netherlands MoD

RIGHT: Convoys ferrying food and ammunition to the frontline will still be needed, with huge batteries required to power these lorries.
US DoD

countermeasures to screen for IEDs and directing automatic sustained fire from a self-loading remote machine gun. In this configuration it can be directed to move ahead of a patrol, while in separate scenarios it can be tasked on its own to conduct reconnaissance surveillance while the operator monitors from distance. The logistics and medical evacuation capabilities are seen as critical in reducing the need for heavy vehicles laden with supplies or flying in helicopters to airlift wounded in heavily contested areas.

In Afghanistan in 2006, an isolated British Army forward operating base at the town of Musa Qaleh in northern Helmand needed to be resupplied. The area was dominated by Taliban forces and insurgents repeatedly tried to shoot down helicopters. A major mission, codenamed Operation Snakebite, was mounted to deliver ammunition, water, and food with a convoy of lorries escorted by a battalion of soldiers. The aim of the UGV is to reduce both risk and resources in situations such as this.

In 2024, British soldiers travelled to the Mojave Desert in California to take part in a series of combat evaluations with the new UGVs. Called Project Convergence Capstone, the aim of the war games was to define how British and US troops would fight a future conflict using autonomous platforms for offensive and resupply missions. During the six-week trial, the UGVs were deployed in various scenarios including in urban areas, listed by the military as Fighting in Built-up Areas (FIBUA) while

projects, while the UK armed forces formed the Army's Experimental and Trials Group (ETG) in 2022 with the Yorkshire Regiment at the heart of it. While these robotic solutions are not yet fully in service with western forces, the Israeli Defence Force (IDF) has already deployed unmanned platforms. During the second incursion into Jabalia camp in Gaza in May 2024, the Israeli army deployed tracked robots for the first time. The IDF said these UGVs were used to clear obstacles by firing blast charges, but Palestinians claimed they killed hundreds of innocent civilians. Meanwhile, in Ukraine, Kyiv's forces are using UGVs with mounted machine guns to attack Russian adversaries, as well as for deception operations.

Across US, British and NATO forces, the primary aim is to use UGVs as a force multiplier, enhancing the safety and endurance of a patrol by fitting the UGV with electronic

RIGHT: A convoy of US Marines Stryker vehicles.
US DoD

being covered by an autonomous Robotic Platoon Vehicles (RPVs). The ETG deployed a robotics and autonomous systems-enhanced battlegroup, including engineers, artillery, electronic warfare (EW) assets and UAVs.

UGVs

UGVs will change the format of modern tactical warfare and is regarded by many senior officers as one of the biggest advances to reduce risk and project power at a time when infantry forces are facing a new threat from above, from drones.

UGVs can move into high-risk areas, monitor enemy forces and, if needed, engage them with remote-controlled machine guns. Future devices will provide high levels of reconnaissance and tactical superiority, giving commanders the ability to effectively combine manned assets with unmanned ground vehicles, a concept known as manned-to-unmanned teaming. Equipped with advanced sensors, cameras, and weaponry, UGVs can execute complex missions with high precision. Their capabilities can be tailored to specific tasks, ranging from bomb disposal and logistics support to engaging enemy targets.

A key requirement for UGVs is to mount surveillance using advanced sensors to provide intelligence of the battlefield. UGVs can also help identify areas of concern with their live-stream cameras, as well as highlight unexpected obstacles and hazards. Small platoon support vehicles, which can carry eight soldiers or stores, provide huge scope to reduce risk to infantry **»**

LEFT: Small all-terrain vehicles will be easy to convert to electric power according to experts. US DoD

LEFT: Unmanned vehicles have taken part in wargames alongside drones and heavy combat vehicles. US DoD

LEFT: Armed UGVs have been used in Ukraine to suppress enemy fire and mount deception operations. UK MoD

BELOW: Unmanned platforms that can be sent directly to a grid reference to deliver supplies or evacuate wounded are a key role in the future. US DoD

and provide information to allow commanders to scope routes for an assault by follow-on forces. The British Army is experimenting with a concept in which these unarmed platforms are directed forward to collate intelligence for reconnaissance forces, which is passed back to larger strike brigades. These UGVs can be wheeled or tracked depending on the terrain and provide live day and night footage of their advance.

Almost silent, EV vehicles are only limited by obstacles or enemy forces. In some scenarios, UGVs have been deployed at scale in test exercises to create a deception and diversion attack. Such deployments have been used in Ukraine, where Ukrainian forces have used UGVs with mannequins dressed in unform and strapped to the vehicles to hoodwink Russian forces. In future conflicts, UGVs could be deployed ahead of a patrol to provide real-time information and situational awareness to the commander, using electronic countermeasures to identify IEDs.

The introduction of the UGV will make a major tactical innovation to military operations and change the manner in which commanders mount attacks and plan offensives. They are seen by many senior officers as having the potential to deliver massive change to combat operations in the same manner as the concept of the creeping artillery barrage in World War One. At the start of World War One, timepieces

ABOVE: US Marines rearm a UGV during war games. USMC

RIGHT: Small tracked UGVS have been used in trials to evacuate wounded soldiers over short distances. US DoD

BELOW: The US military has numerous projects underway with small UGVs. US DoD

RIGHT: A US Marine programmes a UGV before deploying it on a reconnaissance mission. USMC

were mainly a display of wealth and gender classification – women wore wristwatches and men used pocket watches. The introduction of the pocket watch began in the late 19th Century as a tactical tool worn by Army officers to synchronise operations. Traditional bombardment was predictable, but not effective against bunkers, and provided German forces ample time to return to cover before Allied forces reached the front lines. A creeping barrage executed with meticulous timing to synchronise the firing provided a

BELOW: Belarus has developed large wheeled UGVs, although their capability is unclear. Belarus govt

defensive screen for the advancing infantry. The creeping barrage was used at the Battle of Vimy Ridge on April 12, 1917, ensuring a victory for Canadian forces.

The potential roles of the UGV are vast, but while western scientist deploy new concepts, the Chinese and Russian military are also developing products. China is pioneering its commercial technology to support military capability. In 2018, it unveiled the UBot, a small tracked UGV designed for explosive ordnance disposal (EOD) but now being trialled

as a platoon support vehicle. Prior to the war in Ukraine, Moscow's future robotics programme was moving ahead at pace. The Russian defence industry was working on a number of UGV projects that spanned compact, light, mid-sized and heavy vehicles for demining, logistics and combat operations. Between 2016 and 2021, the Russian military fielded some of these as remote-controlled demonstrators.

The Russian Uran-9 robotic armed vehicle entered military service in January 2019 and was first used in a defence exercise in August 2021. It is a tracked UGV promoted as a reconnaissance, surveillance and infantry support platform. The Uran-9 was first deployed during the Syrian civil war, although it functioned poorly according to a performance report by the 3rd Central Research Institute of the Ministry of Defence of the Russian Federation. Nevertheless, Uran-9 vehicles took part in Russia's Victory Parade in 2022; carried on the back of a truck with their sensors and cameras removed

In February-March 2023, Russian state media highlighted the impending test of the Marker UGV in the Donbas region of eastern Ukraine, with this trial conducted not by official members of the military but by an affiliated volunteer organisation. The test was supposed to include » a combat scenario with anti-tank weapons, along with fielding the device as a stationary ISR platform with a tethered drone. Its notable that no actual follow-ups to such tests were mentioned anywhere in the official Russian state media or pro-Russian Telegram channels that had advertised Marker's arrival. It's entirely possible that plans for Marker's 2023 testing were delayed when FPV drones and ISR-tactical drone combos proved not quite as ubiquitous and deadly across the front. Given its relatively large size, Marker could have been an easy prey for UAVs and, if any tests were conducted, they may have been done in relative secrecy and in a controlled setting. As of May 2024, there is no further information about Marker anywhere in the pro-Russian media spaces that report daily from the war.

What was mentioned in the Russian state media was the BRG-1, a transport and evacuation UGV used in Ukraine in limited numbers, mounted with a remote-controlled light machine gun

(LMG). Russian sources have suggested potential future use of artificial intelligence (AI). Another Russian UGV allegedly used in Ukraine is

the SEM-350 multifunctional tracked platform to evacuate wounded soldiers and deliver supplies.

The challenges

Climate change poses a looming danger to national defence as changing weather patterns threaten water supplies. The need to replace diesel fuel and other traditional energy sources is being driven largely by the demand to reduce fossil fuel use. In the High North, Russia is establishing new bases in a race to secure mineral and oil resources in areas of extreme arctic conditions.

Batteries drain very quickly in temperatures dropping to -40°C and the military is seeking alternatives to lithium-ion. These powerful batteries rely on critical minerals that are sourced from a vulnerable supply chain, largely controlled by China. As a consequence, military scientists in the US and UK are seeking alternative sources of power. One potential system being explored to meet the growing operational demands of the military is sodium-based batteries. Sodium-ion batteries are a type of rechargeable battery that work in a way similar to lithium batteries but carry the charge using sodium ions (Na+) instead of lithium ions (Li+). Sodium is a soft, silvery alkaline metal that is very abundant in nature – in sea salt or in the earth's crust. They are less toxic than other popular batteries, as they do not require lithium, cobalt, copper or nickel that can release polluting gases in the event of a fire. And they can be adapted for different uses. Despite their performance, sodium batteries are relatively new on the commercial scene. The mass application of this type of energy storage is still weak due to the lack of an established industrial supply chain and the high cost.